The WESTMINSTER ASSEMBLY AND ITS WORK

GREAT CHRISTIAN BOOKS
LINDENHURST, NEW YORK

The WESTMINSTER ASSEMBLY AND ITS WORK

BENJAMIN B. WARFIELD

Great Christian Books
is an imprint of Rotolo Media
160 37th Street Lindenhurst, New York 11757
(631) 956-0998

Warfield, Benjamin Breckinridge, 1851 - 1921
The Westminster Assembly and Its Work/ by Benjamin B. Warfield
p. cm.
A "A Great Christian Book" book
GREAT CHRISTIAN BOOKS an imprint of Rotolo Media
ISBN 978-1-61010-047-2
Recommended Dewey Decimal Classifications: 200, 238, 270
Suggested Subject Headings:
1. Religion—Christianity—Creeds & catechisms
2. History of Christianity & Christian church
I. Title

Book and cover design are by Michael Rotolo, www.michaelrotolo.com. This book is typeset in the Minion typeface by Adobe Inc. and is quality-manufactured on acid-free paper stock. To discuss the publication of your Christian manuscript or out-of-print book, please contact us.

Manufactured in the United States of America

CONTENTS

FIRST ARTICLE[1]

The "Westminster Assembly of Divines" derives its name from the ancient conventual church of Westminster Abbey, situated in the western district of the county of London. It was convened in the most ornate portion of this noble fabric, the Chapel of Henry VII, on the first day of July, 1643; but, as the cold weather of autumn came on, it was transferred (October 2, 1643) to a more comfortable room (the so-called "Jerusalem Chamber") in the adjoining Deanery. In that room it thereafter sat, not merely to the end of the 1163 numbered sessions, during which its important labors were transacted (up to February 22, 1649), but through some three years more of irregular life, acting as a committee for the examination of appointees to charges and applicants for licensure to preach. It ultimately vanished with the famous "Long Parliament" to which it owed its being. The last entry in its Minutes is dated March 25, 1652.[2]

The summoning of the Westminster Assembly was an important incident in the conflict between the Parliament and the King, which was the form taken on English soil by the ecclesiastico-political struggle by which all Europe was convulsed during the seventeenth century. It was the difficult task of that century to work out to its legitimate issue what had been auspiciously begun in the great revolution of the preceding period; to secure from disintegration what had been won in that revolution; to protect it from reaction; and to repel the destructive forces set in motion against it by the counter-reformation. The new Protestantism was, during this its second age, cast into a crucible in the heats of which it everywhere suffered serious losses, even though it emerged from them, wherever it survived, in greater compactness and purity. The form which the struggle took in England was determined by the peculiar course the Reformation movement had followed in that country. There, on its official side, the Reformation was fundamentally a contest between the King and the Pope. The purpose which Henry VIII set before himself was to free the State from foreign influences exerted by the Pope through the Church; and his efforts were directed, with great singleness of aim, to the establishment of his own authority in ecclesiastical matters to the exclusion of that of the Pope. In these efforts he had the support of Parliament, always jealous of foreign interference; and was not merely sustained but urged on by the whole force of the religious and doctrinal reform gradually spreading among the people, which, however, he made it his business rather to curb than to encourage. The removal of this curb during the reign of Edward VI concealed for a time the evils inherent in the new powers assumed by the throne. But with the accession of Elizabeth, who had no sympathy whatever with religious enthusiasm, they began to appear; and they grew ever more flagrant under her successors. The authority in ecclesiastical matters which had been vindicated to the throne over against the Pope, was increasingly employed to establish the general authority of the throne over against the Parliament. The Church thus became the instrument of the crown in compacting its absolutism; and the interests of civil liberty soon rendered it as imperative to break the absolutism of the King in ecclesiastical affairs as it had ever been to eliminate the papacy from the control of the English Church.

The controversy was thus shifted from a contest between Pope and King to a contest between King and Parliament. And as the cause of the King had ever more intimately allied itself with that of the prelatical party in the Church, which had grown more and more reactionary until under the leading of Laud (1573-1645) it had become aggressively and revolutionarily so,[3] the cause of Puritanism, that is of pure Protestantism, became ever more identical with that of the Parliament. When the parties were ultimately lined up for the final struggle, therefore, it was King and prelate on the one side, against Parliament and Puritan on the other.[4] The main issue which was raised was a secular one, the issue of representative government over against royal absolutism. This issue was fought to a finish, with the ultimate result that there were established in England a constitutional monarchy and a responsible government. There was complicated with this issue, however, also the issue, no doubt, at bottom, of religious freedom over against ecclesiastical tyranny, for it was impatience with ecclesiastical tyranny which gave its vigor to the movement. But the form which was openly taken by the ecclesiastical issue was rather that of a contest between a pure Protestantism and Catholicizing reaction. It was in the mind of neither of the immediate contestants in the main conflict to free the Church from the domination of the State: they differed only as to the seat of the civil authority to which the Church should be subject—whether King or Parliament.

This fundamental controversy lay behind the conflict over the organization of the subject Church and the ordering of its forms of worship—matters which quickly lost their importance, therefore, when the main question was settled. It can occasion little surprise, accordingly, that, when the heats of conflict were over and exhaustion succeeded effort, the English people were able to content themselves, as the ultimate result on the ecclesiastical side, with so slight a gain as a mere act of toleration (May 24, 1689).

This struggle had reached its acutest stage when "the Long Parliament" met, on the third of November, 1640. Profoundly distrustful of the King's sincerity, and determined on its own behalf to be trifled with no longer, Parliament was in no mood for compromises with respect whether to civil or to ecclesiastical affairs. On the ecclesiastical side it was without concern, indeed, for doctrine. It was under no illusions, to be sure, as to the doctrinal significance of the Catholic reaction, and it was fully sensible of the spread of Arminianism in high places.[5] But although there were not lacking hints of such a thing, Tract No. 90 had not yet been written,[6] and the soundly Reformed character of the Church of England as well in its official Articles of Religion as in its general conviction was not in dispute. John Milton accurately reflects the common sentiment of the day when he declares that "in purity of Doctrine" English Churchmen "agreed with their Brethren," that is, of the other Reformed Churches, while yet in discipline, which is "the execution and applying of Doctrine home," they were "no better than a Schisme, from all the Reformation, and a sore scandall to them."[7] What the nation in Commons assembled was determined to be rid of in its Church establishment was, therefore, briefly, "bishoprics" and "ceremonies"—what Milton calls "the irreligious pride and hateful tyranny of Prelates" and the "sencelesse ceremonies" which were only "a dangerous earnest of sliding back to Rome." The Convocation of 1640, continuing illegally to sit after the dissolution of the "Short Parliament," had indeed endeavored to protect the established organization of the Church. It had framed a canon, requiring from the whole body of the clergy the famous "et cetera oath," a sort of echo and counterblast to the "National Covenant" which had been subscribed in Scotland two years before (February 28, 1638). By this oath every clergyman was to bind himself never to give his consent "to alter the government of this Church by archbishops, bishops, deans, and archdeacons, etc., as it stands now established, and as by right it ought to stand."[8] It was even thought worth while to prepare a number of petitions for Parliament with the design of counteracting the effect of this act of convocation. The most important of these, the so-called "London" or "Root and Branch" petition, bore no fewer than 15,000 signatures; and the personal attendance of some 1500 gentlemen of quality when it was presented to Parliament lent weight to its prayer. This was to the effect that "the government of archbishops and lord bishops, deans, and archdeacons, etc." (the same enumeration, observe, as in the "et cetera oath") "with all its dependencies, roots and branches, may be abolished, and all laws in their behalf made void, and the government according to God's word may be rightly placed amongst us."[9] Parliament, however, was in no need of prodding for this work, though it was for various reasons disposed to proceed leisurely in it. The obnoxious Act of Convocation was at once taken up and rebuked. But even the Root and Branch Petition, which was apparently ready from the beginning of the session,[10] was not presented until December 11, and after its presentation was not taken into formal consideration by the House until the following February. As was natural, differences of opinion also began to manifest themselves, as to precisely what should be done with the bishops, and as to the precise form of government which should be set up in the Church after they had been dealt with. There is no reason to doubt the exactness of Baillie's information[11] that the Commons were by a large majority of their membership for erecting some kind of Presbyteries," and "for bringing down the Bishop in all things, spiritual and temporal, so low as can be with any subsistance." In Parliament as out of it the great majority of leading men had become Presbyterian in their tendencies, and the Independents were for the present prepared to act with them. But there was very little knowledge abroad among the members of Parliament of what Presbytery really was,[12] and even the most convinced Presbyterians doubted the feasibility of setting up the whole Presbyterian system at once, while an influential party still advocated what Baillie calls[13] a "calked Episcopacie."[14] It still hung in the balance, therefore, whether bishops should be utterly abolished; and any hesitation which may have existed in the Commons was more than matched in the House of Lords. Above all it never entered the thought of Parliament to set up in the Church any manner of government whatever over which it did not itself retain control.[15] The result was that actual legislation dragged. Abortive bill after abortive bill was brought in; now simply to deprive the prelates of secular functions, and again to abolish the whole Episcopal system. It was not until the autumn of 1641 (October 21), that at length a bill excludingthe bishops from secular activities was passed by the Commons to which the assent of the Lords was obtained (February 5, 1642); [16] and not until another year had slipped away that, under Scotch influence (August, 1642), a bill was finally passed (January 26, 1643) abolishing prelacy altogether.

Alongside of these slowly maturing efforts at negative legislation there naturally ran a parallel series of attempts to provide a positive constitution for the Church after the bishops had been minished or done away. It was recognized from the beginning that for this positive legislation the advice of approved divines would be requisite.[17] Preparation for it took, therefore, much the form of proposals for securing such advice. From all sides, within Parliament and without it alike, the suggestion was pressed that a formal Synod of Divines should be convened to which Parliament should statedly appeal for counsel in all questions which should occasionally arise in the process of the settlement of the Church. And from the beginning it was at least hinted that, in framing its advice, such a Synod might well bear in mind wider interests than merely the internal peace of the Church of England; that it might, for example, consider the advantage of securing along with that a greater harmony with the other Reformed Churches, particularly the neighboring Church of Scotland. It was accordingly with this wider outlook in mind that the proposition was given explicit shape in "the Grand Remonstrance" which was drawn up in the Commons on November 8, 1641, and, having been passed on November 22, was presented to the King on December 1. This document began by avowing the intention of Parliament to "reduce within bounds that exorbitant power which the prelates had assumed unto themselves," and to set up a juster "discipline and government in the Church." It proceeded thus (§ 186): "And the better to effect the intended reformation, we desire there may be a general synod of the most grave, pious, learned, and judicious divines of this island; assisted with some from foreign parts, professing the same religion with us, who may consider of all things necessary for the peace and good government of the Church, and represent the results of their consultations unto the Parliament, to be there allowed of and confirmed, and receive the stamp of authority, thereby to find passage and obedience throughout the kingdom."[18] In pursuance of this design, the Commons engaged themselves desultorily from the ensuing February (1642) in preparations for convening such a Synod. The names of suitable ministers to sit in it were canvassed; selection was made of two divines from each English and one from each Welsh county, two from the Channel Islands and from each University, and four from London;[19] and a bill was passed through both Houses (May 9 to June 30, 1642) commanding the Assembly so constituted to convene on July 1, 1642.[20] The King's assent failing, however, this bill lapsed, and was superseded by another to the same general effect, and that by yet another, and yet another, which went the same way, until finally a sixth bill was prepared, read in the Commons as an ordinance on May 13, 1643, and having been agreed to by the Lords on June 12, 1643, was put into effect without the King's assent. By this ordinance,[21] the Divines, in number 121, supplemented by ten peers and twenty members of the House of Commons (forty being a quorum) were required "to meet and assemble themselves at Westminster, in the Chapel called King Henry the VII's Chapel, on the first day of July, in the year of our Lord One thousand six hundred and forty-three," and thereafter "from time to time [to] sit, and be removed from place to place" and to "confer and treat among themselves of such matters and things, touching and concerning the Liturgy, Discipline, and Government of the Church of England, or the vindicating and clearing of the doctrine of the same from all false aspersions and misconstructions, as shall be proposed unto them by both or either of the said Houses of Parliament, and no other; and to deliver their opinions and advices of, or touching the matters aforesaid, as shall be most agreeable to the word of God, to both or either of the said Houses, from time to time, in such manner and sort as by both or either of the said Houses of Parliament shall be required; and the same not to divulge, by printing, writing, or otherwise, without the consent of both or either House of Parliament."

The prominence given in this ordinance to the reorganization of the government of the Church of England as the primary matter upon which the Assembly thus instituted should be consulted was inherent in the nature of the case, but should not pass without specific notice. And, we should further note, next to the reorganization of the government of the Church the reform of its liturgy was, as was natural in the circumstances, to be the Assembly's care. Doctrinal matters lay wholly in the background. In the heading of the ordinance it is described with exactness as an ordinance "for the calling of an Assembly of learned and godly Divines, and others, to be consulted with by the Parliament, for the settling of the Government and Liturgy of the Church of England"; while it is only added as something clearly secondary in importance that its labors may be directed also to the "vindicating and clearing of the doctrine of the said Church from false aspersions and interpretations." In the body of the ordinance the occasion of calling such an Assembly is detailed. It was because "many things remain in the Liturgy, Discipline, and Government of the Church, which do necessarily require a further and more perfect reformation than as yet hath been attained"; and more specifically because Parliament had arrived at the determination that the existing prelatical government should be taken away as evil, "a great impediment to reformation and growth of religion, and very prejudicial to the state and government of this kingdom." The prime purpose for calling the Assembly is therefore declared to be "to consult and advise" with Parliament, as it may be required to do, in the Parliament's efforts to substitute for the existing prelatical government of the Church, such a government "as may be most agreeable to God's holy word, and most apt to procure and preserve the peace of the Church at home, and nearer agreement with the Church of Scotland, and other Reformed Churches abroad." It is a clearly secondary duty laid on it also "to vindicate and clear the doctrine of the Church of England from all false calumnies and aspersions." It has already been pointed out, that this emphasis on the reformation first of the government and next of the liturgy of the Church, merely reflects the actual situation of affairs. The doctrine of the Church of England was everywhere recognized as in itself soundly Reformed, and needing only to be protected from corrupting misinterpretations; its government and worship, on the other hand, were conceived to be themselves sadly in need of reformation, in the interests of adjustment to the will of God as declared in Scripture, and of harmonizing with the practice of the sister Reformed Churches. Of these sister Reformed Churches, that of Scotland is particularly singled out for mention as the one into "a nearer agreement" with the government of which it were especially desirable that the new government of the Church of England should be brought. But this appears on the face of the ordinance merely as a measure of general prudence and propriety—there is nothing to indicate that any formal uniformity in religion with Scotland was to be sought. It was with the reorganization of the Church of

England alone that Parliament was at this time concerned; and the Assembly called "to consult and advise" with it in this work, had no function beyond the bounds of that Church.

What is of most importance to observe in this ordinance, however, is the care that is taken to withhold all independent powers from the Assembly it convened and to confine it to a purely advisory function. Parliament had no intention whatever of erecting by its own side an ecclesiastical legislature to which might be committed the work of reorganizing the Church, leaving Parliament free to give itself to the civil affairs of the nation. What it proposed to do, was simply to create a permanent Committee of Divines which should be continuously accessible to it, and to which it could resort from time to time for counsel in its prosecution of the task of reconstituting the government, discipline, and worship of the Church of England.[22] Parliament was determined to hold the entire power, civil and ecclesiastical alike, in its own hands; and it took the most extreme pains to deny all initiation and all jurisdiction to the Assembly of Divines it was erecting,[23] and to limit it strictly to supplying Parliament with advice upon specific propositions occasionally submitted to it. The ordinance is described in its heading as an ordinance for the calling of an Assembly "to be consulted with by the Parliament." And in the body of the ordinance the function of the Divines is described as "to consult and advise of such matters and things, touching the premises"- that is to say, the Liturgy, Discipline, and Government of the Church, together with the clearing and vindicating of its doctrine—"as shall be proposed unto them by both or either of the Houses of Parliament, and to give their advice and counsel therein to both or either of the said Houses, when, and as often as they shall be thereunto required." And again, with perhaps superfluous but certainly significant emphasis, in the empowering clauses, the assembled Divines are given "power and authority, and are hereby likewise enjoined, from time to time during this present Parliament, or until further order be taken by both the said Houses, to confer and treat among themselves of such matters and things, touching and concerning the Liturgy, Discipline, and Government of the Church of England, or the vindicating and clearing of the doctrine of the same from all false aspersions and misconstructions, as shall be proposed unto them by both or either of the said Houses of Parliament, and no other"; and are further enjoined "to deliver their opinions and advices of, or touching the matters aforesaid, as shall be most agreeable to the word of God, to both or either of the said Houses, from time to time, in such manner and sort as by both or either of the said Houses of Parliament shall be required; and the same not to divulge, by printing, writing, or otherwise, without the consent of both or either House of Parliament." To make assurance trebly certain the ordinance closes with this blanket clause: "Provided always, That this Ordinance, or any thing therein contained, shall not give unto the persons aforesaid, or any of them, nor shall they in this Assembly assume to exercise any jurisdiction, power, or authority ecclesiastical whatsoever, or any other power than is herein particularly expressed." The effect of these regulations was of course to make the Westminster Assembly merely the creature of Parliament. They reflect the Erastian temper of Parliament, which, intent though it was upon vindicating the civil liberty of the subject, never caught sight of the vision of a free Church in a free State, but not unnaturally identified the cause of freedom with itself and would have felt it a betrayal of liberty not to have retained all authority, civil and ecclesiastical alike, in its own hands as the representatives of the nation. With it, the great conflict in progress was that between King and Parliament; and what it was chiefly concerned with was the establishment of Parliamentary government. In its regulations with respect to the Westminster Assembly, however, it did not go one step beyond what it had been accustomed to see practised in England with regard to the civil control of ecclesiastical assemblies. The effect of these regulations was, in fact, merely to place this Assembly with respect to its independence of action, in the same position relatively to Parliament, which had been previously occupied by the Convocations of the Church of England relatively to the crown, as regulated by 25 Henry VIII (1533/4), c. 19, revived by 1 Eliz. (1558/9), c. 1. s. z., and expounded by Coke, "Reports," xiii. p. 72.[24] And it must be borne in mind that stringent as these regulations were, they denied to the Assembly only initiation and authority: they left it perfectly free in its deliberations and conclusions.[25] The limitation of its discussions to topics committed to it by Parliament, moreover, proved no grievance, in the face of the very broad commitments which were ultimately made to it; and its incapacity to give legal effect to its determinations—which it could present only as "humble advices" to Parliament—deprived them of none of their intrinsic value, and has in no way lessened their ultimate influence.

In pursuance of this ordinance, and in defiance of an inhibitory proclamation from the King, the Assembly duly met on July 1, 1643. It was constituted in the Chapel of Henry VII after there had been preached to its members in the Abbey by Dr. William Twisse, who had been named by Parliament prolocutor to the Assembly, a sermon which was listened to by a great concourse, including both Houses of Parliament. Sixty-nine members were in attendance on the first day; and that seems to have thereafter been the average daily attendance.[26] No business was transacted on this day, however, but adjournment was taken until July 6: and it was not until July 8 that work was begun, after each member had made a solemn protestation "to maintain nothing in point of doctrine but what 'he believed' to be most agreeable to the Word of God, nor in point of discipline, but what may make most for God's glory and the peace and good of his church." The first task committed to the Assembly was the revision of the Thirty-nine Articles, and it was engaged upon this labor intermittently until October 12, at which date it had reached the sixteenth Article.[27] That the Assembly was thus put for its first work upon the least pressing of the tasks which were expected of it—"the vindicating and clearing of the doctrine of the Church of England from all false aspersions and misconstructions"—may have been due to the concurrence of many causes. It may have been that in its engrossment with far more immediately pressing duties than even the settlement of the future government of the Church of England, Parliament had had no opportunity to prepare work for the Assembly. Beyond question, however, the main cause was the premonition of that change in the posture of affairs by which the work of the Assembly was given a new significance and a much wider range than were contemplated when it was called, and an international rather than a merely national bearing. It was natural that Parliament should hold it back from its more important labors until the arrangements already in progress for this change in the scope of its work were perfected. It is not necessary to suppose that the determinations of the Assembly were essentially altered—or that Parliament supposed they would be—by the change in the bearing of its work to which we allude. It is quite true that in the course of the debates which were subsequently held, sufficient confusion of mind was occasionally exhibited on the part of many in the Assembly to make us thankful that these debates were actually regulated by the firm guidance of men of experience in the matters under discussion.[28] But the known convictions of the members of the Assembly, evidenced in their printed works no less than in the debates of the Assembly, render it altogether unlikely that had they been called upon, as it was at first contemplated they should be, to advise Parliament unassisted and merely with respect to the settlement of the Church of England, they would have failed to fight their way to conclusions quite similar to those they actually reached.[29] Nevertheless the alteration of the bearing of their work from a merely national to international significance, obviously not only gave it a far wider compass than was at first contemplated, but quite revolutionized its spirit and threw it into such changed relations as to give it a totally different character.

This great change in the function which the Assembly was to serve, was brought about by the stage reached by the civil conflict in the summer of 1643. The Parliamentary cause had sunk to its lowest ebb; and it had become imperative to obtain the assistance of the Scots. But the assistance of the Scots could be had only at the price of a distinctively ecclesiastical alliance. The Scotch had been far greater sufferers than even the English from the absolutism which had been practised by the Stuart Kings in ecclesiastical matters. Not content with asserting and exercising original authority in the ecclesiastical affairs of England, these monarchs had asserted and were ever increasingly exercising the same absolutism in the ecclesiastical affairs of Scotland also; and had freely employed the ecclesiastical instruments at their service in England in order to secure their ends in Scotland. But the relations of Church and State in Scotland were not quite the same as those which obtained in England.[30] In the northern kingdom, from the beginning of the Reformation, the ideal of a free Church in a free State had been sedulously cherished and repeatedly given effect; and the government of the Church was in representative courts which asserted and exercised their own independent spiritual jurisdiction. The interference of the King with the working of this ecclesiastical machinery was, therefore, widely resented as mere tyranny. And as it was employed precisely for the purpose of destroying the ecclesiastical organization which had been established in the Church of Scotland, and of assimilating the Scottish Church in government and mode of worship (doctrine was not in question[31]) to the model of the Church of England, which was considered by the Scots far less pure and Scriptural than their own, it took the form also of religious persecution. No claim could be put in here, as was put in in England, that the royal prerogative was exercised only for conserving the ancient settlement of the Church. It was employed precisely for pulling down what had been built up, and was, therefore, not only tyrannical in form but revolutionary in its entire effect. Add that it was understood that the instrument, if not the instigator, of this persecuting tyranny had come in late years to be a foreign prelate aggressively bent even in England on a violently reactionary policy, to which that nation was unalterably averse, and in Scotland balking apparently at nothing which promised to reduce the Church there to the same Catholicizing model which he had set himself to establish and perpetuate in England, and it will be apparent how galling the situation had become. Chafing under such wrongs, Scotland needed only a spark to be set on fire. The spark was provided in the spring of 1637, by the imposition upon the Church of Scotland by the mere proclamation of the King—"without warrant from our Kirk," as say the Scottish Commissioners—of a complete new service-book designed to assimilate the worship of the Scottish Church as closely as possible to that of England, or, as Milton expresses it from the English Puritan point of sight,[32] "to force upon their Fellow-Subjects, that which themselves are weary of, the Skeleton of a Masse-Booke."[33] When the book was read in the Cathedral Church of St. Giles, Edinburgh, July 23, 1637, however "incontinent," says Baillie,[34] "the serving-maids began such a tumult, as was never heard of since the Reformation in our nation"; and thus "the serving-maids in Edinburgh"—symbolized in the picturesque legend of Jennie Geddes and her stool, which has almost attained the dignity of history—"began to draw down the Bishop's pride, when it was at the highest."[35] The movement thus inaugurated ran rapidly forward: as Archbishop Spottiswoode is said to have exclaimed, "all that they had been doing these thirty years past was thrown down at once." The Scots immediately reclaimed their ecclesiastical, and, in doing that, also their civil liberties; eradicated at once every trace of the prelacy which had been imposed on them, and restored their Presbyterian government; secured the simplicity of their worship and reinstated the strictness of their discipline; and withal bound themselves by a great oath—"the National Covenant"[36]—to the perpetual preservation of their religious settlement in its purity.

The Scots to whom the English Parliament made its appeal for aid in the summer of 1643, were, then, "a covenanted nation." They were profoundly convinced that the root of all the ills they had been made to suffer through two reigns, culminating in the insufferable tyranny of the Laudian domination, was to be found in the restless ambition of the English prelates; and they had once for all determined to make it their primary end to secure themselves in the permanent peaceful possession of their own religious establishment. The Parliamentary Commissioners came to them, indeed, seeking aid in their political struggle and with their minds set on a civil compact: they found the Scots, however, equally determined that any bond into which they entered should deal primarily with the ecclesiastical situation and should be fundamentally a religious engagement. "The English," says Baillie,[37] "were for a civill League, we for a religious Covenant." The Scots, indeed, had nothing to gain from the alliance which was offered them, unless they gained security for their Church from future English interference; while on the other hand by entering into it they risked everything which they had at such great cost recovered for themselves. Their own liberties were already regained; the cause of Parliament in England, on the contrary, hung in the gravest doubt. It really was an act of high chivalry, to call it by no more sacred name, for them to cast in their lot at this crisis with the Parliament; and more than one Scot must have cried to himself during the ensuing years, "Surelie it was a great act of faith in God, and hudge courage and unheard of compassion, that moved our nation to hazard their own peace, and venture their lives and all, for to save a people so irrecoverablie ruined both in their owne and all the world's eyes."[38] On the other hand, the Scots demanded nothing more than that the Parliament should explicitly bind itself to the course it was on its own account loudly professing to be following, and had already declared, in the ordinance (for example) by which it had called to its aid an advisory council of Divines,[39] to be the object it was setting before itself in the reconstruction of the English Church. All that was asked of the Parliament, in point of fact, was, thus, that it should give greater precision, and binding force under the sanction of a solemn covenant, to its repeatedly declared purpose. That the Parliamentary Commissioners boggled over this demand, especially if it were in the effort to keep "a doore open in England to Independencie,"[40] was scarcely worthy of them, and boded ill for the future. That they yielded in the end and the Scots had their way may have been, no doubt, the index of their necessities; but it would seem to have been already given in the logic of the situation. To hold out on this issue were to stultify the whole course of the Long Parliament heretofore. The result was, accordingly, "The Solemn League and Covenant."

By this pact, the two nations bound themselves to each other in a solemn league and covenant, the two terms being employed apparently as designating the pact respectively from the civil and the religious sides. This "league and covenant" was sworn to in England by both Houses of Parliament, as also by their servant-body, the Assembly of Divines, and in Scotland by both the civil and religious authorities; and then was sent out into the two countries to be subscribed by the whole population. By the terms of the engagement made in it, the difference in the actual ecclesiastical situations of the contracting parties was clearly recognized, and that in such terms as to make the actual situation in Scotland the model of the establishment agreed upon for both countries. The contracting parties bound themselves to "the *preservation* of the reformed religion in the Church of Scotland, in doctrine, worship, discipline, and government, against our common enemies," on the one hand; and on the other to "the *reformation* of religion in the kingdoms of England and Ireland,[41] in doctrine, worship, discipline, and government, according to the word of God and the example of the best reformed Churches"; to the end that thereby "the Churches of God in the three kingdoms" might be brought "to the nearest conjunction and uniformity in religion, confession of faith, form of Church government, directory for worship and catechizing."[42] According to the terms of this engagement, therefore, the Parliament undertook, in the settlement of the Church of England on which it was engaged, to study to bring that Church to the nearest possible "conjunction and uniformity" with the existing settlement of the Church of Scotland, and that in the four items of Confession of Faith, Form of Church Government, Directory for Worship, and Catechizing; and these four items were accordingly currently spoken of thereafter as "the four points or parts of uniformity."[43] By this engagement there was given obviously not only a wholly new bearing to the work of the Assembly of Divines which had been convened as a standing body of counsellors to the Parliament in ecclesiastical affairs, and that one of largely increased significance and heightened dignity; but also a wholly new definiteness to the work which should be required of it, with respect both to its compass and its aim. Whatever else Parliament might call on the Assembly to advise it in, it would now necessarily call on it to propose to it a new Form of Church Government, a new Directory for Worship, a new Confession of Faith, and a new Catechetical Manual. And in framing these formularies the aim of the Assembly would now necessarily be to prepare forms which might be acceptable not merely to the Church of England, as promising to secure her internal peace, and efficiency, but also to the Church of Scotland as preserving the doctrines, worship, discipline, government already established in that Church. The significance of the Solemn League and Covenant was, therefore, that it pledged the two nations to uniformity in their religious establishments and pledged them to a uniformity on the model of the establishment already existing in the Church of Scotland.

The taking of the Solemn League and Covenant by the two nations, on the one side marked the completeness of the failure of the ecclesiastical policy of the King, and on the other seemed to promise to the Scots the accomplishment of a dream which had long been cherished by them. The broader ecclesiastical policy consistently pursued by the throne throughout the whole Stuart period had been directed to the reduction of the religion of the three kingdoms to uniformity.[44] The model of this uniformity, however, was naturally derived from the prelatical constitution of the Church of England, to which the Stuart monarchs had taken so violent a predilection; and that, in the later years of their administration when the policy of "thorough" was being pushed forward, as interpreted in an extremely reactionary spirit. No one could doubt that important advantages would accrue from uniformity in the religious establishment of the three kingdoms; and the Scots, taking a leaf out of their adversaries' book, began early to press for its institution in the reconstructed Church, on the basis, however, of their own Presbyterianism. Their motive for this was not merely zeal for the extension of their particular church order, which they sincerely believed to be *jure divino*; but a conviction that only so could they secure themselves from future interference in their own religious establishment from the side of the stronger sister-nation. They had no sooner recovered their Presbyterian organization, and simplicity of worship, therefore, than they began to urge the reformation of the sister-church on their model. The Scottish peace-commissioners, for example, took up to London with them, in the closing months of 1640,[45] a paper drawn up by Alexander Henderson, in which they set forth their "desires concerning unity in religion," and "uniformity of Church government as a special mean to conserve peace in his majesty's dominion."[46] In this paper they declared that it is "to be wished that there were one Confession of Faith, one form of Catechism, one Directory for all the parts of the public worship of God, and for prayer, preaching, administration of sacraments, etc., and one form of Church government, in all the Churches of his majesty's dominions." Here we see enumerated the precise schedule of uniformity which was afterwards undertaken under the sanction of the Solemn League and Covenant, the items being arranged climactically in the order of ascending immediate importance. For the Commissioners recognized that it was uniformity of Church Government which was most imperatively required; and equally frankly urged that this uniformity of Church Government should be sought by the common adoption by both nations of the Presbyterian system. The propriety of such a demand they argued on the grounds that the Presbyterian system was the system in use in all other Reformed Churches; that the English prelatical system had been the source of much evil; that the Reformed Churches were clear that their system is *jure divino*, while the *jus divinum* was not commonly claimed for Episcopacy;[47] and above all, that the Scotch were bound by oath, not lately taken in wilfulness but of ancient obligation, to the Presbyterian system, while the English were free to recast their system, and indeed were already bent on recasting it. This paper was handed in to the Lords of the Treaty on March 10, 1641, with little apparent immediate effect. Indeed, there seems to have been even a disposition to resent its suggestions. The whole matter was put to one side by the Parliament with a somewhat grudging word of thanks to Scotland for wishing uniformity of Church Government with England, and a somewhat dry intimation that Parliament had already taken into consideration the reformation of Church Government and would proceed in it in due time as should "best conduce to the glory of God and peace of the Church."[48] This response was accordingly embodied in the treaty of August 7, 1641,[49] to the effect that the desire expressed for "a conformity of Church Government between the two Nations" was commendable; "and as the Parliament hath already taken into consideration the reformation of Church Government, so they will proceed therein in due time as shall best conduce to the glory of God and peace of the Church and of both Kingdomes."

Nevertheless the suggestion ultimately bore fruit. It was repeated by Henderson to the Scottish Assembly, meeting at the end of July next ensuing, in a proposition that the Scotch Church, by way of holding out the olive branch, should itself draw up a new "Confession of Faith, a Catechisme, a Directorie for all the parts of the publick worship, and a Platforme of Government, wherein possiblie England and we might agree."[50] This proposal met so far with favor that Henderson was himself appointed to take the labor in hand, with such help as he should choose to call to his side. On further consideration, however, he himself judged it best to await the issue of affairs in England;[51] fully recognizing that the adoption of purely Scottish forms by both nations was not to be hoped for, but if uniformity was ever to be attained, "a new Forme must be sett downe for us all, and in my opinion some men sett apairt sometime for that worke."[52] Accordingly, when, as the outbreak of open war between the Parliament and the King became imminent in the midsummer of 1642, Parliament addressed a letter to the Scottish Assembly declaring "their earnest desyre to have their Church reformed according to the word of God,"[53] and their well-grounded hope of accomplishing this task if war could be averted—all of which was interpreted, and was intended to be interpreted, by an accompanying letter "from a number of English ministers at London" in which it was asserted that "the desire of the most godly and considerable part" among them was for the establishment in England of the Presbyterian Government, "which hath just and evident foundation both in the Word of God and religious reason"; and, referring directly to the Scottish proposal, "that (according to your intimation) we may agree in one Confession of Faith, one Directorie of Worship, one publike Catechisme, and form of Government"[54]—the Assembly naturally responded[55] by reiterating its desire for this unifying settlement and renewing "the Proposition made by" its Commissioners in 1641 "for beginning the work of Reformation at the Uniformity of Kirk-Government." "For what hope," the Assembly argues, "can there be of Unity in Religion, of one Confession of Faith, one Form of Worship, and one Catechism, till there be first one Form of Ecclesiastical Government?" The response of Parliament,[56] satisfactory if a little reserved, intimated the expected meeting of the reforming Synod on November 5, and asked the appointment of some Scottish delegates "to assist at" it;[57] a request which was immediately complied with, and the Commissioners named, who, a year later, after the adoption of the Solemn League and Covenant, went up in somewhat different circumstances, and with a somewhat different commission.[58]Meanwhile the Scots assiduously kept their proposals for the institution of uniformity of religious constitution in the two nations forward,[59] and the course of events finally threw the game into their hands, when the Commissioners of Parliament appeared in Edinburgh in August, 1643, seeking Scottish aid in their extremity, and swore the Solemn League and Covenant as its price. By this compact the two nations bound themselves precisely to the punctual carrying out of the program proposed by the Scottish Commissioners in 1640-1641.

The Solemn League and Covenant, it must be borne in mind, was no loose agreement between two Churches, but a solemnly ratified treaty between two nations. The Commissioners who went up to London from Scotland under its provisions, went up not as delegates from the Scottish Church to lend their hand to the work of the Assembly of Divines, but as the accredited representatives of the Scottish people, to treat with the English Parliament in the settlement of the details of that religious uniformity which the two nations had agreed with one another to institute. They might on the invitation of the English Parliament be present at the sessions of the advisory Assembly it had convened, and give it their advice throughout all the processes of its deliberations. And it is obvious that their presence there would much advance the business in hand, by tending to prevent proposals of a hopelessly one-sided character from being formulated. It would seem obvious also that it was eminently fitting that Scotch counsels should be heard in the deliberations of a body to which, under whatever safeguards, was in point of fact committed the task of preparing the drafts of formularies which it was hoped might prove acceptable to both Churches—especially when thirty members of the English Parliament, the party of the other part to this treaty, were members of the body. But the proper task of the Scotch Commissioners lay not in the Assembly of Divines, but outside of it. It was their function, speaking broadly, to see that such formularies were proposed to the two contracting nations for the reducing of their church establishments to uniformity, as would be acceptable to the Church of Scotland which they represented, and would fulfil the provisions of the Solemn League and Covenant under the sanction of which they were acting.[60] And if the Assembly of Divines were utilized, as it in point of fact was utilized, to draw up these draft formularies, it was the business of the Scottish Commissioners to see that the Divines did their work in full view of the Scottish desires and point of view, and that the documents issued from their hands in a form in which the Church of Scotland could adopt them. In the prosecution of these their functions as Treaty Commissioners, their immediate relations were not with the Assembly of Divines but with the Parliament or with whatever commissioners the Parliament might appoint to represent it in conference with them. They could treat with or act directly upon the Assembly of Divines only at the request of Parliament, to treat with which they were really commissioned; and only to the extent which Parliament might judge useful for the common end in view. A disposition manifested itself; it is true, on their appearing in London, to look upon them merely as Scotch members of the Assembly of Divines, appointed to sit with the Divines in response to a request from the English Parliament. This view of their functions they vigorously repudiated. They were perfectly willing, they said,[61] to sit in the Assembly as individuals and to lend the Divines in their deliberations all the aid in their power, if the Parliament invited them to do so. But as Commissioners for their National Church, they were Treaty Commissioners, empowered to treat with the Parliament itself. Accordingly a committee of Parliament was appointed (October 17-20, 1643) to meet statedly with them and consult with them, to which was added a committee from the Divines; and it was through this "Grand Committee" that the work of the Assembly on the points of uniformity was directed.[62] As they were requested by Parliament also "as private men" to sit in the Assembly of Divines they occupied a sort of dual position relatively to the Assembly,[63] and this has been the occasion of some misunderstanding and even criticism of their varied lines of activity. The matter is, however, perfectly simple. In all its work looking to the preparation of a basis for the proposed uniformity, the Assembly really did its work under the direction proximately not of the Parliament but of "the Grand Committee," and the results of its labors were presented, therefore, not merely to Parliament, but, also, through its Commissioners, to the Scottish Assembly. The Scotch Commissioners as members of "the Grand Committee" had therefore an important part in preparing the work of the Divines for them in all that concerned the uniformity; and as present at the deliberations of the Divines were naturally concerned to secure for their own proposals favorable consideration, and did their best endeavors to obtain such results as they might as Commissioners of the Scotch Church recommend to its approval. Throughout everything they acted consistently as the Commissioners of the Scotch Church, seeking the ends which they were as such charged with securing. They were not members of the Assembly of Divines, were present at its meetings and took part in its deliberations only by express invitation and frankly as the agents of the Scotch Church, and possessed and exercised no voice in the determinations of the body.[64]

By the Solemn League and Covenant, therefore, the work of the Assembly of Divines was revolutionized, and not only directed to a new end but put upon a wholly new basis. Its proceedings up to the arrival of the first of the Scottish

Commissioners in London, on September 15, 1643, and the taking of the Covenant on September 25th, must be regarded simply as "marking time." The Parliament perfectly understood before the first of July, what was before it; and it could never have imagined that the revision of the Thirty-nine Articles upon which it had set the Assembly could prove an acceptable Confession of Faith for the two Churches. The employment of the Assembly in that labor was but an expedient to occupy it innocuously until its real work under the new conditions could be begun. With the coming of the Scotch Commissioners, however, the real work of the Assembly became possible, and was at once committed to it. Already on September 18, there was referred to it from the Commons the consideration of a discipline and government apt to procure nearer agreement with the Church of Scotland and of a new liturgical form, and from the 12th of the October following,[65] when the Lords had concurred, the Assembly was engaged, with many interruptions, no doubt, but in a true sense continuously, and even strenuously, upon the "four things mentioned in the Covenant, viz.: the Directory for Worship, the Confession of Faith, Form of Church Government, and Catechism."[66] And when "the debating and perfecting" of these four things were over, the real work of the Divines was done, and the last of the Scotch Commissioners accordingly, having caused a formal Minute to that effect to be entered on the records of the Assembly, felt able to take leave of the Assembly and return home.[67] As an advisory committee to the Parliament of England, many other tasks were laid on the Assembly, some of which had their close connection with its work on the points of uniformity, and some of which had no connection with it at all. And the life of the Assembly was prolonged as such a committee for many months after its whole work on "the uniformity" had been completed. But its significant work lies decidedly in its preparation of a complete set of formularies—Confession, Catechisms, Platform of Government, Directory for Worship—which it proposed to the contracting nations as a suitable basis for a uniform church establishment in the three kingdoms.

In the Second Article[68] some account will be given of the work of the Divines in the preparation of these formularies.

SECOND ARTICLE[69]

In the First Article some account was given of the calling of the Westminster Assembly and of its historical meaning. It was pointed out that its really significant work was the preparation of formularies designed to serve the Churches of the three kingdoms as a basis for uniform establishments. Some account of its work on these so-called "four parts of uniformity" is now to be given.

Of these "four parts of uniformity" the one which was at once the most pressing and the most difficult for the Assembly was the preparation of a platform of government for the Churches. Both Parliament and Assembly were, indeed, fairly committed to the Presbyterian system under solemn sanction; and the majority of the members of both bodies were sincerely Presbyterian in conviction.[70] But sincerity and consistency are very different matters; and so soon as the details of church organization were brought under discussion, a bewildering variety of judgments was revealed. The Scots, though prepared to yield in the interest of harmony all that it was possible to yield, perhaps more than it was altogether wise to yield, were yet peremptory for a really Presbyterian establishment, as they were bound to be under the engagements of the National Covenant and were fully entitled to be under those of the Solemn League and Covenant. In this they were supported by the overwhelming majority of the Assembly. It fell, indeed, to the lot of the Scots to hold back the English Presbyterians from precipitate and aggressive action. It was their policy to obtain if possible a settlement not so much imposed by a majority as at least acceptable to all.[71] They therefore gave themselves not merely to conciliate the minor differences which emerged in the debate—on the part of those, for example, who preferred a mixed Presbyterian and Episcopal system (Twisse, Gataker, Gouge, Palmer, Temple)—but even "to satisfy" the small but able band of Independents in the Assembly (Goodwin, Nye, Burroughs, Bridge, Carter, Caryl, Phillips, Sterry), who wished all authoritative government in the Church to stop with the congregation. The Independents, on their part, adopted an obstructive policy, and set themselves not only to obtain every concession it was possible to wring from the majority, but to delay the adoption of its scheme of Presbyterian government, and if possible, to defeat its establishment altogether. They were supported in this policy by the Erastians who, though not largely represented in the Assembly (Lightfoot, Coleman, Selden), were dominant in Parliament,[72] which accordingly showed itself ultimately averse to establishing any church government possessed of independent or final jurisdiction even in spiritual matters.[73] In the vain hope of escaping the schism threatened by the Independents and of avoiding an open breach with the Erastian Parliament, the Presbyterian majority in the Assembly proceeded slowly with their platform of government, contenting itself meanwhile with debating and voting a series of detached propositions, which were moreover couched in the simplest and most comprehensive language, while they postponed for the present framing a systematic statement. This delay was, however, itself as great an evil as could have been encountered; and as the differences it was hoped to conciliate were such as in their nature were not subject to "accommodation," the Assembly was compelled in the end to report its scheme of government, which it had thus reduced to its lowest terms and in so doing shorn of much of its strength and attractiveness, in the face of the protest of the Independents and to a determinedly Erastian Parliament.[74]

The first portion of the Assembly's work presented to Parliament was the "Directory for Ordination" which was sent up on April 20, 1644.[75] This was followed the ensuing autumn (November 8 and December 11, 1644) by certain "Propositions concerning Church Government," compacted out of the several separate declarations upon points of government which had from time to time been voted by the Assembly in the course of its debates, now gathered together and thrown into some semblance of order. It must be confessed that the work of collecting and ordering these propositions was somewhat carelessly done. Now and then, for example, in transferring them from the Minutes clauses are retained which have no proper meaning in their new setting. We are told, for instance, that "the pastor is an ordinary and perpetual officer in the church, prophesying of the time of the Gospel"; and it is only from the *vidimus* of the votes of the Assembly preserved by Gillespie that we learn that the clause "prophesying of the time of the Gospel," here sheer nonsense, was a comment on Jer. iii. 15-17 which was on this ground adduced as a proof-text for the proposition "that there is such an ordinary and perpetual officer in the church as a pastor."[76] Again there is enumerated among the offices of a pastor as if it were an independent function, "to dispense other divine mysteries"; and we have to go to Gillespie's *vidimus* to learn that the Assembly meant just the Sacraments (along with the benediction) and no "other divine mysteries" by this phrase.[77] The document nevertheless contains a firm enough, though cautiously worded, presentation of the essentials of the Presbyterian system; and was therefore followed, of course, by a protest from the Independent members of the Assembly, which naturally occasioned a reply from the Assembly itself. These documents were later (1648) published together under the title, "The Reasons Presented by the Dissenting Brethren Against Certain Propositions Concerning Church Government, together with the Answers of the Assembly of Divines to these Reasons of Dissent"; and republished in 1652 under the new title, "The Grand Debate concerning Presbytery and Independency by the Assembly of Divines convened at Westminster by authority of Parliament."

The "Propositions" themselves, to which the "Directory for Ordination" was adjoined, so as to form a single document, were dealt with very freely by Parliament. Intent only on the practical settlement of the Church while it preserved to itself all ecclesiastical as well as civil authority, Parliament on the one hand, undertook to extract from "The Propositions" only so much of a practical directory as would enable the Church to go on; and on the other, precipitated the Assembly of Divines into what threatened to become endless debates on the *jus divinum* of the details of the Presbyterian system and the autonomy of the Church and particularly the right of the Church in the exercise of its own spiritual jurisdiction to exclude the scandalous from participation in the Lord's Supper.[78] In these debates, and in the whole conduct of its negotiations with Parliament during this dispute, the Assembly manifested the highest dignity, firmness, and courage. If Parliament utterly refused to set up a series of ecclesiastical courts with independent jurisdiction even in purely spiritual matters, and insisted on reserving to itself, or to secular committees established by and directly responsible to it, the review of even such spiritual functions as the determination of fitness to receive the Sacrament of the Lord's Supper,[79] the Assembly on its part respectfully but firmly protested against such an intrusion of the secular arm into spiritual things, and refused to be a party to any ecclesiastical arrangement which denied to the Church what it deemed its divinely prescribed rights and responsibilities. It took for its motto the ringing phrase, "The Crown rights of Jesus Christ," and declared that on His shoulders the government is, and that all power in heaven and earth has been given Him, and, ascended far above all heavens, He has received gifts for His Church and has given to it officers necessary for its edification and the perfecting of His saints. It showed itself, in the noble words of Warriston, "tender, zealous and carefull to assert Christ and his Church their priviledge and right... that Christ lives and reigns alone over and in his Church, and will have all done therin according to his Word and will, and that he hes given no supreme headship over his Church to any Pope, King, or Parliament whatsoever."[80] On the matter of the spiritual jurisdiction of the Church, the Assembly remained unmoved and insisted that Christ has instituted in the Church a government and governors ecclesiastical distinct from the civil magistrates.[81]Meanwhile, realizing that it was of the first importance to get the framework of the Presbyterian government established and in operation, the Divines under the leadership of Alexander Henderson, passing by these doctrinal matters for the moment, had drawn up a "Practical Directory for Church Government," which they had presented to Parliament July 7, 1645. In this document, which avoided as far as possible all questions of principle, very full and definite expositions were given of the actual framework of Presbyterian government. It commended itself in this aspect of it to Parliament and was ultimately in large part adopted by it in an ordinance passed on August 29, 1648, and was published in this somewhat diluted shape as "The Form of Church Government to be used in the Church of England and Ireland."

In Scotland this document was never formally approved, as the earlier "Propositions," which were approved by the General Assembly of the Church of Scotland, were never ratified by the English Parliament. Thus neither became of authority in both Churches. The modified Presbyterianism set up by the Long Parliament in England, under the direction of the one document, moreover, was soon swept away; while the other document, approved indeed by the Scottish General Assembly but never ratified by the Estates of the Scottish Parliament, though it has held its place among the formularies of the Scottish churches until today, has been largely superseded in the churches deriving their descent from them. The permanent influence of the labors of the Westminster Assembly in the great matter of church organization—supposed at the time, as they were, to be its most important, as they certainly were its most pressing and its most difficult labors—has been largely unofficial and somewhat indirect. It has doubtless been exerted nearly as powerfully, indeed, through such treatises as "The Grand Debate," already mentioned, or the "Jus Divinum Regiminis Ecclesiastici," published by some of the ministers of London at the end of 1646, but supposed to incorporate the Assembly's answers to the *jus divinum* queries propounded to it by Parliament, as through their formal advices to Parliament. Indeed, it is questionable whether the really great works of individual members of the Assembly on these topics, such as Gillespie's "An Assertion of the Government of the Church of Scotland" (1641) and "Aaron's Rod Blossoming" (1646), Rutherford's "Due Right of Presbytery" (1644), and Henderson's "The Government and Order of the Church of Scotland" (1641, and again 1690), must not be conceived the chief vehicles of this influence. The most that can be said for the formal work of the Assembly in this field is that it gave ungrudgingly an immense amount of self-denying labor to preparing advices for the use of Parliament in settling the government of the Church of England on a Presbyterian model, but was prevented by the circumstances in which it did its work from doing full justice in these documents either to its own clear and strong convictions or to the system with which it was dealing.

Next to the elaboration of a new scheme of government for the Church of England which should bring it into harmony with the established government of the Church of Scotland, the most pressing task committed to the Assembly of Divines was the preparation of a new form of worship to take the place of "The Book of Common Prayer" now to be abolished, by which the modes of worship in the Church of England should be conformed "to the example of the best Reformed Churches." The prosecution of this task was attended with no such difficulties as beset the formulation of the scheme of government. There existed no doubt differences enough in usage and preference among the several parties in the Assembly in this region of church life also; and these differences ranged all the way from a distaste among the Independents to all prescriptions in worship to a predilection in the case of some of the English churchmen for a complete liturgy.[82] But they were less deeply rooted and more easily conciliated in a middle way than the differences by which they were divided in the matter of church government. The work of formulating forms of worship acceptable to all was, therefore, pushed through comparatively rapidly, and the whole "Directory for the Publique Worship of God throughout the Three Kingdoms of England, Scotland, and Ireland" was sent up to Parliament by the end of 1644. By an ordinance of Parliament, dated January 3d, [4th], 1645, it was established in England and Wales to "be henceforth used, pursued, and observed,... in all Exercises of the Publique Worship of God, in every Congregation, Church, Chappell, and place of Publique Worship"; and a month later it was approved and established in Scotland by Acts of Assembly (February 3d) and the Estates of Parliament (February 6th). After some slight adjustments it was printed and put into circulation in both countries during the ensuing spring (the English edition bears on its titlepage the date 1644, but that is "old style"). As is indicated by the title, the book is not "a straight liturgy," but a body of agenda and paradigms. Some of these paradigms, to be sure, are so full that they are capable of being transmuted into liturgical forms by a mere transposition of their clauses into the mode of direct address, but they were not intended to be so employed and are too compressed to lend themselves readily to such use.[83]

The first draft of the document was prepared by a subcommittee of the Great Treaty Committee, and, as in the case of the "Practical Directory for Church Government," it was largely the work of the Scots.[84] The suggestions for the prayers of the Sabbath-day service, and for the administration of the Sacraments, were in the first instance their work;[85] and they ultimately had the drawing up also of the suggestions for preaching and for catechizing.[86] Naturally, therefore, there is much in the book which is derived from Scottish usage. The Sabbath service, for example, is in its general structure practically identical with that of the "Book of Common Order" (commonly called "Knox's Liturgy"), and the materials for the consecration prayer in the directory for celebrating the Lord's Supper are mainly derived from the same source. But, on the other hand, the latter part of this same prayer and the concluding thanksgiving are more reminiscent of the English "Book of Common Prayer."[87] The book as a whole, in fact, does not so much follow Scottish as offer a compromise between Scottish and Puritan usage. Acquiescence in this compromise must have cost the Scots a great effort, as it was, in effect, a reversal of a deliberate policy which had been adopted by the Scottish Church. After the recovery of its purity of worship consequent upon the outbreak of 1637, the Scottish Church was considerably disturbed by the intrusion of certain "novations" into its worship, which were really Puritan customs, seeping in, no doubt, in part, from England, but mainly brought in by returning Scottish emigrants to Ulster. These "novations" were made the subject of earnest conference at the General Assembly of 1641, and again at that of 1643; and, in order to meet the peril which they appeared to threaten, it was determined at the latter Assembly that "a Directorie for the worship of God" should "be framed and made ready, in all the parts thereof, against the next General Assembly" (that of 1644), Henderson, Calderwood, and Dickson being charged with the drafting of it. This whole undertaking was naturally superseded, however, by the inauguration of the broader attempt to introduce, through the mediation of the Westminster Assembly, a common Directory for the three kingdoms. But the odd effect of this supersession was that the "novations" for the exclusion of which from the Church of Scotland the first undertaking was set on foot, were in large measure constituted the official usage of the Church by the new Directory. By the very conditions of its formulation this Directory became a compromise between the Scottish and the Puritan modes of worship rather than a bar to the introduction into Scotland of Puritan modes of worship.

By these "novations" the use of "read prayers,"[88] and even of the Lord's Prayer, in public worship, was discountenanced, as was also the use of the Gloria Patri, and of the Apostles' Creed in the administration of the Sacraments, and the habit of the minister to bow in silent prayer upon entering the pulpit. No one of these usages, on which the Scots laid much stress, except the use of the Lord's Prayer, is prescribed by the Directory; but as none of them are proscribed either, the Scots were able to "save their face" by attaching to the Act by which the Assembly adopted the Directory the proviso: "That this shall be no prejudice to the order and practice of this Kirk, in such particulars as are appointed by the Books of Discipline and Acts of General Assemblies, and are not otherwise ordered and appointed in the Directory." By a supplementary Act of the same Assembly, however, they voluntarily laid aside—"for satisfaction of the desires of the reverend Divines in the Synod of England, and for uniformity with that Kirk, so much endeared to us"—the "lawful custom" of "the Minister's bowing in the pulpit."[89] Of more importance than any of these usages, at least for the conduct of the public services, was the loss by the Scots, through the Westminster Directory, of the office of "Reader." From the Reforniation down, the former or liturgical portion of the Scottish Sabbath service—the opening prayer, the lessons from Scripture, and the singing of a Psalm—had been conducted by a "Reader," the Minister taking charge of the services, and indeed commonly entering the church, only when he ascended the pulpit to preach. The Westminster Divines found no Scriptural warrant for the office of "Reader," and, much against the wishes of the Scots, enacted that the Minister should conduct the entire service. "Reading of the Word in the Congregation," they set down in their Directory, "being part of the Public Worship of God (wherein we acknowledge our dependence upon Him, and subjection to Him), and one means sanctified by Him for the edifying of His people, is to be performed by the Pastors and Teachers."[90] The only exception they would allow was that they permitted candidates for the ministry occasionally to perform the office of reading, as also that of preaching, on permission of their Presbyteries.

On the other hand, besides the general structure of the services, as already noted, Scottish usage was followed in the Directory in many important points. This was particularly true in the regulations for the celebration of the Sacraments. The Baptismal service, for example—although the Creed, the Lord's Prayer, and godparents were omitted—yet followed in general the Scotch order; and it was thought a great gain for the Scots when, in opposition to practically the universal English custom, they got it ordained that Baptism was never to be administered in private, but always in "the place of Public Worship, and in the face of the Congregation." It was over the mode of celebrating the Lord's Supper, however, that the most strenuous debates were held. The manner of celebrating that rite prevalent among the Independents, seemed to the Scots to be bald even to irreverence; while many of the details of the Scottish service were utterly distasteful to the extremer Puritans. In the end, things were ordered fairly to the satisfaction of the Scots, although in one matter which they thought of very great importance, they were ultimately compelled to content themselves with an ambiguous rubric. This concerned the place and manner of the reception of the elements. The Scots were insistent for their own custom, in which the communicants arranged themselves at the table and served one another with the elements as at an actual meal. This usage was, after strenuous debate, at last ordered: but the rubric was subsequently so changed that it ultimately read, merely: "The Table... being so conveniently placed, that the Communicants may orderly sit about it, or at it." Accordingly the Scotch Assembly, in adopting the Directory, added this proviso: "That the clause in the Directory of the Administration of the Lord's Supper, which mentioneth the Communicants sitting about the Table, or at it, be not interpreted as if, in the judgment of this Kirk, it were indifferent, and free for any of the Communicants not to come to, and receive at the Table; or as if we did approve the distributing of the Elements by the Minister to each Communicant, and not by the Communicants among themselves." In a supplementary Act the Assembly further laid down a series of details for the administration of this Sacrament. It was in accordance with the Scottish usage, also, that in a concluding section, the Directory abolished all Festival days, and affirmed that "there is no day commanded in Scripture to be kept holy under the Gospel but the Lord's Day, which is the Christian Sabbath."[91]

A document formed as this was by a series of compromises was not very likely to command the hearty loyalty of any section of its framers. We are not surprised, therefore, that it was much neglected in England, though in Scotland it gradually made its way against ancient custom and ultimately very much molded the usages of the churches. Even in Scotland, however, this gradually perfected assimilation to the Directory has of late suffered from some reaction; and in some of the churches deriving their formularies from the Scottish Church, the Directory was early superseded by new models of their own.[92] At this distance of time we may look upon it dispassionately; and, so viewed, it can scarcely fail to commend itself as an admirable set of agenda, in spirit and matter alike well fitted to direct the public services of a great Church. It is notable for its freedom from petty prescriptions and "superfluities" and for the emphasis it places upon what is specifically commanded in the Scriptures. Its general tone is lofty and spiritual; its conception of acceptable worship is sober and restrained and at the same time profound and rich; the paradigms of prayers which it offers are notably full and yet free from overelaboration, compressed and yet enriched by many reminiscences of the best models which had preceded them; and it is singular among agenda for the dominant place it gives in the public worship of the Church to the offices of reading and preaching the Word.[93] To both of these offices it vindicates a place, and a prominent place, among the parts of public worship, specifically so called, claiming for them distinctively a function in inducing and expressing that sense of dependence on God and of subjection to Him in which all religion is rooted and which is the purest expression of worship; and thus justifying in the ordering of the public services of the churches the recognition of the Word as a means, perhaps we should say the means, of grace. It expends as much care upon the minister's proper performance of the offices of reading and preaching the Word, therefore, as upon his successful performance of the duty of leading the congregation in prayer and acceptably administering to it the Sacraments. The paragraph on the Preaching of the Word is in effect, indeed, a complete homiletical treatise, remarkable at once for its sober practical sense and its profound spiritual wisdom, and suffused with a tone of sincere piety, and of zeal at once for the truth and for the souls which are to be bought with the truth.

One of the sections of the Directory is given to the Singing of Psalms, and declares it "the duty of Christians to praise God publickly, by Singing of Psalms together in the Congregation, and also privately in the family." This rubric manifestly implied the provision of a Psalm Book, and it was made part of the function of the Assembly in preparing a basis for uniformity of worship in the Churches of the three kingdoms, to supply them with a common Psalm Book. The way was prepared for this by the submitment to the Assembly by the House of Commons on November 20, 1643, of the query whether "it may not be useful and profitable to the Church, that the Psalms set forth by Mr. Rouse, be permitted to be publickly sung." The result of the Assembly's examination of Mr. Rouse's version (first printed in 1643) was to recommend it, after it had been subjected to a thorough revision at its own hands, to Parliament as a suitable Psalm Book for the Church (autumn of 1645). The Commons accordingly ordered the book printed in this revised form (it appeared in 1646, i.e. February, 1647), and (April 15, 1646) issued an order establishing it as the sole Psalm Book to be used in the Churches of England and Wales, though the House of Lords never concurred in this order. The Scotch Assembly subjected the book to a still further and more searching revision, and by an act passed in 1649 (ratified by the Estates of Parliament in 1650) approved it in this new form for use in the

Scottish churches. It is in this Scottish revision alone (printed in 1650), in which they can only by courtesy continue to bear the name of Francis Rouse as their author, that these Psalms have passed into wide use.[94]

To the punctual completion of "the third part of uniformity," that is to say, the preparation of a new Confession of Faith for the contracting Churches, the Divines were urged by no immediately pressing necessity in the situation of the Church of England. The existing Thirty-nine Articles were recognized by them as a soundly Reformed Creed, the doctrine of which required only to be vindicated and cleared from the false interpretations which the reactionary party was already endeavoring to foist upon it. With the internal needs of the Church of England alone in view, they might possibly have felt contented with a simple revision of these Articles, somewhat more thorough than that they had been engaged upon early in their labors.[95] The duty of preparing an entirely new Creed was imposed on them solely by the Solemn League and Covenant, by which a common Confession of Faith was made one of the bases of the uniformity in religion which the contracting nations had bound themselves to institute. It was not supposable that either Church would be content simply to accept and make its own the existing Creed of the other. Indeed, neither Church possessed a Creed which it could seriously propose to the other as suitable to the purpose or adequate to the needs of the times. The old Scotch Confession of 1560, breathing as it does the fervor of the Reformation era and full of noble expressions as it is, is too much of an occasional document, too disproportionate in its development of its topics, and too little complete in its scope or precise in its phraseology to serve as the permanent expression of the faith of a great and comprehensive Church;

and the new Confession brought forward by the prelatical party in 1616, though sound in doctrine and in parts finely wrought out, suffered from the same defects. The Scots themselves recognized that they had no Creed which they could ask the English to adopt as the common Confession of the unified Churches, and therefore, when contemplating seeking such unification had it in mind to undertake the preparation of a new Creed for the purpose.[96] There was greater reason for the English to feel similarly with regard to their own formularies. The Thirty-nine Articles had, in their past experience, proved an inadequate protection against the most dangerous doctrinal reactions. It was therefore that the ecclesiastical authorities had been compelled to put forth, a half-century earlier, those "orthodoxal assertions" which have come down to us under the name of the Lambeth Articles (1595). It had long been the desire of the Puritans that these Articles should be set alongside of the Thirty-nine Articles, as an authoritative exposition of their real meaning. This desire had been given expression at the Hampton Court Conference (1604), and had been met in the Church of Ireland by the incorporation of the Lambeth Articles along with the Thirty-nine Articles into those Irish Articles of 1615, to which we may be sure the Westminster Divines would have turned rather than to the Thirty-nine Articles, had they thought of recommending the simple adoption of an existing Creed as the doctrinal standard of the unified Churches, and which indeed they did make the basis of their own new Creed. Since the necessity of a new Creed was a result of the new conditions brought about by the Solemn League and Covenant, therefore, these conditions imposed an absolute necessity for the preparation of such a document; and as time passed on the demand for the accomplishment of the task became ever more urgent. The "woeful longsomeness" of the Assembly in all its work was bringing the fulfilment of the engagements into which the nations had entered into jeopardy, and the Scots, who had paid the price of the Covenant on the faith of the fulfilment of its provisions, not unnaturally began uneasily to urge their more speedy fulfilment. It was accordingly under pressure from Scotland that the Divines at length entered actively upon the accomplishment of this "third part of uniformity."[97]

It must not be inferred, however, from their slowness in entering upon it, that the work of drawing up a Confession of Faith was one uncongenial to the Assembly of Divines; or one for which its members possessed little native fitness or had made little direct preparation; or one which presented for them special difficulties. On the contrary, there was no work committed to them for which they were more eminently qualified, or in which they acquitted themselves with more distinguished success; nor was there any work committed to them in the prosecution of which they were less impeded by differences among themselves. The deep-seated antagonisms which divided them into irreconcilable parties, lay in the region of church organization and government. Doctrinally they were in complete fundamental harmony, and in giving expression to their common faith needed only to concern themselves to state it truly, purely, and with its polemic edges well-turned out towards the chief assailants of Reformed doctrine, in order to satisfy the minds of all. There were indeed differences among them in doctrine, too; but these lay for the most part within the recognized limits of the Reformed system, and there was little disposition to press them to extremes or to narrow their Creed to a party document. To the Amyraldians, of whom there was a small but very active and well-esteemed party in the Assembly (Calamy, Seaman, Marshall, Vines), there was denied, to be sure, the right to modify the statement of the *ordo decretorum* so as to make room for their "hypothetical universalism" in the saving work of Christ (cf. the Confession, iii. 6, viii. 5, 8). But the wise plan was adopted with respect to the points of difference between the Supralapsarians, who were represented by a number of the ablest thinkers in the Assembly (Twisse, Rutherford), and the Infralapsarians, to which party the great mass of the members adhered, to set down in the Confession only what was common ground to both, leaving the whole region which was in dispute between them entirely untouched. This procedure gives to the Confession a peculiar comprehensiveness, while yet it permits to its statements of the generic doctrine of the Reformed Churches a directness, a definiteness, a crisp precision, and an unambiguous clarity which are attained by few Confessional documents of any age or creed. In its third chapter, for example, in which the thorny subject of "God's Eternal Decree" falls for treatment, the Westminster Confession has attained, by this simple method, the culmination of the Confessional statement of this high mystery. Everything merely individual and as well everything upon which parties in the Reformed Churches are divided with respect to this deep doctrine, is carefully avoided, while the whole ground common to all recognized Reformed parties is given, if prudent, yet full and uncompromising statement.

The architectonic principle of the Westminster Confession is supplied by the schematization of the Federal theology, which had obtained by this time in Britain, as on the Continent, a dominant position as the most commodious mode of presenting the *corpus* of Reformed doctrine (so e.g. Rollock, Howie, Cartwright, Preston, Perkins, Ames, Ball, and cf. Dickson's

"Sum of Saving Knowledge" and Fisher's "Marrow of Modern Divinity," both of which emanated from this period and were destined to a career of great influence in the Scottish theology). The matter is distributed into thirty-three comprehensive chapters. After an opening chapter "Of the Holy Scripture" as the source of divine truth—which is probably the finest single chapter in any Protestant Confession and is rivalled in ability only by the chapter on Justification in the Tridentine Decrees—there are successively taken up the topics of God and the Trinity, the Divine Decree, Creation, Providence, the Fall and Sin, and then God's Covenant with Man, and Christ the Mediator of the Covenant, while subsequent treatment is given to the stages in the *ordo salutis* in the order first of the benefits conferred under the Covenant (Vocation, Justification, Adoption, Sanctification) and then of the duties required under the Covenant (Faith, Repentance, Good Works, Perseverance, Assurance). Then come chapters on the Law, Christian Liberty, Religious Worship, Oaths and Vows, followed by others on the relations of Church and State, the Church and the Sacraments, and the rubrics of Eschatology. All the topics of this comprehensive outline are treated with notable fulness, with the avowed object not merely of setting forth the doctrine of the Churches with such clearness and in such detail as to make it plain to all that they held to the Reformed faith in its entirety,[98] but also to meet and exclude the whole mob of errors which vexed the time.[99] In the prosecution of their work as practical pastors protecting and indoctrinating their flocks, the Divines had acquired an intimate acquaintance with the prevailing errors and a remarkable facility in the formulation of the Reformed doctrine in opposition to them, which bore rich fruit in their Confessional labors. The main source of their Confessional statements was, thus, just the Reformed theology as it had framed itself in their minds during their long experience in teaching it, and had worked itself out into expression in the prosecution of their task as teachers of religion in an age of almost unexampled religious unrest and controversy. This work, however, had not been done by them in isolation. It had been done, on the contrary, in the full light of the whole body of Reformed thought. It is idle, therefore, to inquire whether they depended for guidance in the scholastic statement of their doctrine on British or on Continental masters. The distinction was not present to their minds; intercourse between the British and the Continental Reformed was constant, and the solidarity of their consciousness was complete. The vital statement of Reformed thought ripened everywhere simultaneously in the perfect interaction which leaves open no question of relative dependence. The Federal mode of statement, for example, came forward and gradually became dominant throughout the Reformed world at about the same time; and the Westminster Confession owes its preeminence among Reformed Confessions, not only in fulness but also in exactitude and richness of statement, merely to the fact that it is the ripest fruit of Reformed creed-making, the simple transcript of Reformed thought as it was everywhere expounded by its best representatives in the middle of the seventeenth century. So representative is it of Reformed theology at its best, that often one might easily gain the illusion as he read over its compressed sections that he was reading a condensed abstract of some such compend as Heppe's "Dogmatik der evangelisch-reformirten Kirche."

In giving form and order to their statement of the Reformed faith, however, it was but natural for the Westminster Divines to take their starting point from the formularies in most familiar use among themselves. The whole series of Reformed Confessions, as well as all the best Reformed dogmaticians, were drawn upon to aid them in their definitions, and it is possible to note here and there traces of their use. But it was particularly the Irish Articles of 1615, which are believed to have been prepared by Usher, to which they especially turned. From these Articles they derived the general arrangement of their Confession, the consecution of topics through at least its first half, and a large part of the detailed treatment of such capital Articles as those on the Holy Scripture, God's Eternal Decree, Christ the Mediator, the Covenant of Grace, and the Lord's Supper. These chapters might almost be spoken of as only greatly enriched revisions of the corresponding sections of the Irish Articles. Nothing, however, is taken from the Irish Articles without much revision and enrichment, for which every available source was diligently sought out and utilized. There are traces, minute but not therefore the less convincing or significant, for example, of the use for the perfecting of the statements of the Confession, of even the Aberdeen Articles of 1616 and of the Assembly's own revision of the Thirty-nine Articles. So minutely was every phrase scrutinized and every aid within reach invoked.

The work of formulating the Confession of Faith was begun in Committee as early as the midsummer of 1644 (August 20).[100] But it was not until the following spring (April 25, 1645)[101] that any of it came before the Assembly; and not until the next midsummer (July 7, 1645) that the debates upon it in the Assembly began. Time and pains were lavishly expended on it as the work slowly progressed. By the middle of 1646 the whole was substantially finished in first-draft, and the review of it begun. The first nineteen chapters were sent up to the

House of Commons on September 25, 1646, and the entire work on December 4. Proof-texts from Scripture were subsequently added, and the book supplied with them was placed in the hands of Parliament on April 29, 1647. Immediately on its completion the book was carried to Scotland, and by an Act of the General Assembly of 1647, ratified by the Estates of Parliament February 7, 1649, it was constituted the official Creed of the Church of Scotland. Meanwhile action on it dragged in the English Parliament. It was not until June 20, 1648, that, curtailed of chapters xxx. and xxxi., on "Church Censures" and "Synods and Councils," and certain passages in chapters xx. ("of Christian Liberty and Liberty of Conscience"), xxiii. ("of the Civil Magistrate"), and xxiv. ("of Marriage and Divorce"), it was approved by Parliament and printed under the title of "Articles of the Christian Religion"; and not until March 5, 1660, after the interval of the Protectorate, that it was declared by the so-called "Rump Parliament" to be "the public Confession of the Church of England," only to pass, of course, out of sight so far as the Church of England was concerned in the immediately succeeding Restoration.

The book was not one, however, which could easily be relegated to oblivion. Thrust aside by the established Church of England, it nevertheless had an important career before it even in England, where it became the Creed of the Non-Conformists. The Independents, at their Synod, met in 1658 at the Savoy, adopted it in the form in which it had been published by Parliament (1648), after subjecting it to a revision which in no way affected its substance; and the Baptists, having still further revised it and adjusted it to fit their particular views on. Baptism, adopted it in 1677. By both of the bodies it was transmitted to their affiliated co-religionists in America, where it worked out for itself an important history.[102] It was of course also transmitted, in its original form, by the Scotch Church to the Churches, on both sides of the sea, deriving their tradition from it, and thus it has become the Confession of Faith of the Presbyterian Churches of the British dependencies and of America. In the latter it has been adapted to their free position relatively to the State by means of certain alterations in the relevant chapters, and in some of the Churches it has been subjected to some other revisions. It has thus come about that the Westminster Confession has occupied a position of very widespread influence. It has been issued in something like 200 editions in Great Britain and in about 100 more in America.[103] It was rendered into German as early as 1648 (reprinted, somewhat modified, in Böckel's "Bekenntnisschriften der evangelisch-reformirten Kirche," 1847); and into Latin in 1656 (often reprinted, e.g. Niemeyer's "Collectio Confessionum," Appendix, 1840, and Schaff, "Creeds of Christendom," 1878); and into Gaelic in 1725 (often reprinted). More recently it has been translated into Hindustani (1842), Urdu (1848), German (1858), Siamese (1873), Portuguese (1876), Spanish (1880 and again 1896-1897), Japanese (1880), Chinese (1881), Arabic (1883), Gujurati (1888), French (1891), as well as into Benga, Persian, and Korean (as yet in MS.). It thus exists today in some seventeen languages[104] and is professed by perhaps a more numerous body than any other Protestant creed.[105]

The labors of the Divines upon the "fourth part of uniformity," that is to say, in the preparation of a Catechism for the unified Churches, reached a similarly felicitous result. The Westminster Assembly was eminently an assembly of catechists, trained and practised in the art.[106]Not only were its members pupils of masters in this work, but not fewer than a dozen of themselves had published Catechisms which were in wide use in the churches (Twisse, White, Gataker, Gouge, Wilkinson, Wilson, Walker, Palmer, Cawdrey, Sedgewick, Byfield, and possibly Newcomen, Lyford, Hodges, Foxcroft). A beginning was made at a comparatively early date towards drawing up their Catechism; but this labor was successfully completed only after all the other work of the Assembly had been accomplished. In the earlier notices of work on the Catechism it is not always easy to distinguish between references to the preparation of the Directory for Catechising or the Directory for Worship and references to the preparation of the Catechism itself. But as early as November 21, 1644, Baillie speaks of "the Catechise" as already drawn up; and on the 26th of December following, as nearly agreed on in private in its first draft. And we learn from the "Minutes" (p. 13) that on December 2, 1644, a committee was appointed "for hastening the Catechism," and that this committee was augmented on February 7th following (p. 48). On August 5, 1645, the material of this Catechism was under debate in the Assembly itself; and by August 20 it would seem to have been so far nearing completion that a committee was appointed to "draw up the whole draught" of it. Nothing, however, came of this work. It appears, in effect, that one or two false starts were made upon the Catechism before the Divines got down to their really productive work upon it. After midsummer of 1645 we hear nothing about the Catechism for a year, when, writing July 14, 1646, Baillie tells us that all that had been hitherto accomplished was set aside and a new beginning made. "We made, long agoe," he writes, "a prettie progress in the Catechise; but falling on rubbes and long debates, it wes laid aside till the Confession wes ended, with resolution to have no matter in it but what wes expressed in the Confession, which should not be debated over againe in the Catechise."

Accordingly, the Confession being now finished and in process of review, the new Catechism[107] was taken up (September 11), and from September 14, 1646, to January 4, 1647, was rapidly passed through the Assembly up to the questions which dealt with the Fourth Commandment. This, however, was only another false start. In the prosecution of this work, the Assembly became convinced that it was attempting an impossible feat; as the Scottish Commissioners express it,[108] it was essaying "to dress up milk and meat both in one dish." It therefore again called a halt and "recommitted the work, that tuo formes of Catechisme may be prepared, one more exact and comprehensive, another more easie and short for new beginners."[109] Recommencing on this new basis, the "Larger Catechism" began to be debated on April 15, 1647, and was finished on the 15th of the following October, and sent up to Parliament on October 22. The "Shorter Catechism" was taken up on August 5, 1647, seriously taken in hand October 19, began to come into the Assembly on October 21, and was finished November 22 and sent up to Parliament November 25, 1647. The proof-texts for both Catechisms occupied the Assembly from November 30, 1647, to April 12, 1648, and were presented to Parliament April 14, 1648. The "Shorter Catechism" was approved by Parliament on September 22-25, 1648; and issued under the title, "The Grounds and Principles of Religion, contained in a Shorter Catechism (according to the Advice of the Assembly of Divines sitting at Westminster), to be used throughout the Kingdom of England and Dominion of Wales." The "Larger Catechism," however, although passed by the Commons on July 24, 1648, stuck in the House of Lords and never received its authorization. In Scotland, both were approved by acts of the General Assembly of 1648, ratified by the Estates of Parliament, February 7, 1649; but no mention is made of them in the reestablishment of Presbytery after the Revolution. In the later history of the Westminster formularies, the "Larger Catechism" has taken a somewhat secondary place; but no product of the Divines has been more widely diffused or has exercised a deeper influence than their "Shorter Catechism." It at once became in Scotland the textbook in religion in the schools, and has held that position up to today; and for a long period it was scarcely less popular in Non-Conformist England than in Scotland. From both sources it was transmitted to their affiliated Churches in America; and in the extension of the mission work of the several Presbyterian Churches in the nineteenth century its use has been diffused throughout the world.

The tracing of the sources of the Westminster Catechisms is rendered exceptionally difficult not merely by the amazing fecundity in catechetical manuals of the British Churches of the immediately preceding and contemporary periods, but also by the obvious independence of the Westminster Divines in giving form to their catechetical formularies, and their express determination to derive the materials for them, as far as possible, from their own Confession of Faith. The contents of the first Catechism taken in hand by them—the Catechism of 1644-1645—have not been transmitted to us. We may infer, however, from the meager details which have found record, that it was probably based on the Catechism of Herbert Palmer, published in 1640 under the title of "An Endeavour of Making Christian Religion Easie" (5th edition, 1645). The matter of the second Catechism prepared by the Assembly—that of the autumn of 1646—is preserved for us in the Minutes, so far as it was debated and passed by the Assembly.[110] It professedly derives its material as far as possible from the Assembly's Confession of Faith, but as it covers in large part ground not gone over in the Confession, much of its material must have an independent origin. Palmer's Catechism still seems to underlie it, but supplies no material for its exposition of the Commandments; and the influence of the manuals of Usher seems discernible. Much the same must be said of the sources of the Catechisms which the Assembly completed, "Larger" and "Shorter." The doctrinal portion of the "Larger Catechism" is very much a catechetical recension of the Assembly's Confession of Faith; while in its ethical portion (its exposition of the Ten Commandments) it seems to derive most from Usher's "Body of Divinity" and Nicholl's and Ball's "Catechisms"; and in its exposition of the Lord's Prayer to go back ultimately through intermediary manuals to William Perkins' treatise on the Lord's Prayer. The "Shorter Catechism" is so original and individual in its form, that the question of its sources seems insoluble, if not impertinent. It in the main follows the outline of the "Larger Catechism"; but in its modes of statement it now and again varies from it and in some of these variations reverts to the Catechism of the autumn of 1646. In their striking opening questions both Catechisms go back ultimately to the model introduced by Calvin, possibly but certainly not probably through the intermediation of Leo Judae.[111]Perhaps of all earlier Catechisms the little manual of Ezekiel Rogers most closely resembles the "Shorter Catechism" in its general plan and order; but there is little detailed resemblance between the two. After all said, the "Shorter Catechism" is a new creation, and must be considered in structure and contents alike the contribution to the catechetical art of the Westminster Divines themselves.

No other Catechism can be compared with it in its concise, nervous, terse exactitude of definition, or in its severely logical elaboration; and it gains these admirable qualities at no expense to its freshness or fervor, though perhaps it can scarcely be spoken of as marked by childlike simplicity. Although set forth as "milk for babes" and designed to stand by the side of the "Larger Catechism" as an "easie and short" manual of religion "for newbeginners," it is nevertheless governed by the principle (as one of its authors—Seaman—phrased it), "that the greatest care should be taken to frame the answer not according to the model of the knowledge the child hath, but according to that the child ought to have." Its peculiarity, in contrast with the "Larger Catechism" (and the Confession of Faith), is the strictness with which its contents are confined to the very quintessence of religion and morals, to the positive truths and facts which must be known for their own behoof by all who would fain be instructed in right belief and practice.[112] All purely historical matter, and much more, all controversial matter—everything which can minister merely to curiosity, however chastened—is rigidly excluded. Only that is given which, in the judgment of its framers, is directly required for the Christian's instruction in what he is to believe concerning God and what God requires of him. It is a pure manual of personal religion and practical morality.

To whom among the Westminster Divines we more especially owe these Catechetical manuals—and particularly the "Shorter Catechism"—we have no means of determining. It is, of course, easy to draw out from the records of the Assembly the names of the members of the committees to which the preparation of the materials for them was entrusted. But this seems to carry us a very little way into the problem. On the whole, Herbert Palmer, who bore the reputation, as Baillie tells us, of being "the best catechist in England," appears to have been the leading spirit in the Assembly in all matters concerned with catechetics: and he apparently served on all important committees busied with the Catechisms up to his death, which occurred, however (August 13, 1647), before the "Shorter Catechism" seems to have been seriously taken in hand. We have no direct evidence to connect him with the authorship of this Catechism, only the first—evidently a purely preliminary—report upon which he was privileged to be the medium of making, and the contents of which certainly show much less resemblance to those of his own manual than there is reason to believe was exhibited by the earliest Catechism undertaken by the Assembly. There is still less reason, of course, to connect with its composition the name of Dr. John Wallis, Palmer's pupil and friend, who attended the committee charged with its review as its secretary (from November 9, 1647), and whose mathematical genius has been thought to express itself in the clear and logical definitions which characterize the document. Dr. Wallis' close connection with the "Shorter Catechism," in the minds of the contemporary and following generations, appears to be mainly due to the publication by him at once on its appearance (1648) of an edition of it broken up into subordinate questions according to the model of the treatise of his friend and patron, Palmer. Still less have we evidence to connect the Scotch Commissioners directly with the composition of the "Shorter Catechism." The record may give us reason to infer that the earliest Catechism undertaken by the Assembly may have been in the first instance drafted by the Scots.[113] But we lack even such faint suggestions in the case of the Catechisms which were ultimately prepared.

Indeed, these Catechisms, and especially the "Shorter," are precisely the portion of the Assembly's constructive work, in the composition of which the Scotch Commissioners appear to have had the least prominent part. Henderson had died before the Confession of Faith was finished; Baillie left immediately after its completion; Gillespie in the midst of the work on the "Larger Catechism"; while Rutherford, who alone remained until the "Shorter Catechism" was under way, judged that his presence until the completion of the "Larger Catechism" justified the declaration that the Scots had lent their aid to the accomplishment of all "the 4 things mentioned in the Covenant,"[114] which is as much as to say that he looked upon the completion of the "Shorter Catechism" as largely a matter of routine work unessential to the main task of the Assembly.[115] It does not follow, of course, that the Scots had nothing to do with the composition of the "Shorter Catechism." We do not know how fully its text had been worked out before any of it was brought before the Assembly, or how hard it rested on previous work done in committee or in the Assembly, or to whom the first essays in its composition were due. Of course, the Scots served with all committees up to the moment of their departure, and may have had much to do with the framing of the drafts of documents with which we have no explicit evidence to connect their names. But they appear to have had less to do with giving the Catechisms their final form than was the case with the other documents prepared by the Divines for the use of the united Churches. The Catechisms come to us preeminently as the work of the Assembly, and we are without data to enable us to point to any individual or individuals to whom we can confidently assign their characteristic features.

With the completion of the Catechisms, the work of the

Assembly under the engagement of the Solemn League and Covenant was done. The Scots, as we have seen, caused a Minute to this effect to be entered upon the records of the Assembly (October 15, 1647), reciting that some of them had given assistance to the Divines throughout the whole of their labors looking to uniformity. And on the return to Scotland of Rutherford, the last of the Scots to leave London, the Commission of the General Assembly dispatched a letter to the Assembly of Divines (November 26, 1647)—with whom it joins in the address "the Ministers of London, and all the other well-affected brethren of the Ministrie in England"—which accurately reflects the state of affairs relatively to the work of the Divines at the end of the year 1647. In this letter the Scots express their unwavering purpose to abide by the Covenant they had sworn, and exhort their English brethren to do the same, noting at the same time the difficulties they saw besetting the way, and recommending in view of them diligence in the fear of God. In pursuance of its covenant engagement, the letter goes on to declare, the Scottish Church had approved and ratified the "Directory for Worship" "being about tuo yeares agoe agreed upon by the Assemblies and Parliaments of both kingdomes," and the "Doctrinal Part of Church Government"—that is, the "Propositions for Church Government" of 1644—"agreed upon by the reverend and learned Assemblie of Divines"; and had also approved the "Confession of Faith" "as sound and orthodox for the matter, and agreed vnto on their part that it be a part of the Vniformity, and a Confession of Faith for the Churches of Christ in the three kingdomes"; while it purposed to consider and expected to approve the "Directory of Church Government," the "Catechism," and the new "Paraphrase of the Psalms" at the next Assembly, to meet in the summer of 1648.

From this statement we perceive how far Scotland had outrun England in fulfilling the terms of their mutual engagement, and how uneasy the northern kingdom was becoming over the ever growing prospect that they would never be fully met in England. Meanwhile all the work of the Divines for uniformity was done; there remained only the completion of the proof-texts for the Catechisms, with the completion of which their entire function, as enlarged and given international significance by the provisions of the Solemn League and Covenant, was performed. We find the Assembly, therefore, on the day on which Rutherford took his leave of it, appointing a committee "to consider of what is fit to be done when the Catechism is finished" (November 9, 1647). For a time the Assembly turned back to the controversies of the great days of its past, with the Independents and the Erastians; to its responses to the *jus divinum* queries;[116] and especially to its answers to the reasons of the Dissenting brethren against the Presbyterian system of government, which it now prepared for publication (1648, and again 1652). It had ceased to have any further function, however, than that of a standing advisory board to Parliament; and as the significance of Parliament decreased ("Pride's purge," December 6, 1648, was the precursor of the end, which came in 1653) its own importance necessarily fell with it. It became increasingly difficult to get a quorum together; and its work dwindled into the mere task of an examining committee for vacant charges, until it passed out of existence with the Parliament from which it derived its being.

What the Divines could do for the institution of the proposed uniformity of religion in the three kingdoms, we see, then, had been done and well done, by the beginning of 1648. The institution of uniformity on the basis formulated by them did not lie within their powers. That was a matter of treaty engagement between the two nations. We have seen that the Scotch were in no way backward in the fulfilment of their part of the engagement. The same cannot be said for England. The political situation was very different at the opening of 1648 from what it had been in midsummer of 1643; and Parliament was now perhaps little inclined, and, to do it justice, was certainly little able, to carry out all it had felt constrained to promise five years before.[117] The rise of Independency to political power and the usurpation of the army were the supersession of the Covenant and all its solemn obligations: and after the usurpation came ultimately, not the restoration of Parliamentary government and Presbyterianism, but the restoration of monarchy and prelacy. The dream of an enforced uniformity of religion in the three kingdoms on a Presbyterian basis, under the inspiration of which the Divines had done their constructive work, had vanished; and so far as the successful issue of their labors depended on alliance with a friendly state, their work, as regards England at least, had failed. But this alliance was not the strength of the Assembly, but its weakness. Its work was not in character political, but religious; and its product needed no imposition by the civil power to give it vitality. Whatever real authority the formularies it had framed possessed, was inherent in them as sound presentations of truth, not derived from extraneous sources. And by the inherent power of their truth they have held sway and won a way for themselves to the real triumph of the voluntary adhesion of multitudes of Christian men. It is honor enough for the Westminster Assembly that it has provided this multitude of voluntary adherents with a practicable platform of representative government on Scriptural lines, and a sober and sane directory of worship eminently spiritual in tone; and above all, with the culminating Reformed Confession of Faith, and a Catechism preeminent for the exactness of its definitions of faith and the faithfulness of its ethical precepts.

ENDNOTES

1. Originally printed in *The Princeton Theological Review*, vi. 1908, pp. 177-210.

2. In the ordinance convening the Assembly, it is commissioned to sit "during this present Parliament, or until further order be taken by both the said houses."

3. "Laud's real influence was derived from the unity of his purpose. He directed all the powers of a clear, narrow mind and a dogged will to the realization of a single aim. His resolve was to raise the Church of England to what he conceived to be its real position as a branch, though a reformed branch, of the great Catholic Church throughout the world.... The first step in the realization of such a theory was the severance of whatever ties had hitherto united the English Church to the Reformed Churches of the Continent.... His policy was no longer the purely conservative policy of Parker and Whitgift; it was aggressive and revolutionary" (J. R. Green, "Short History of the English People," New York, 1877, pp. 499-502).

4. As Mr. J. A. R. Marriott, "The Life and Times of Lucius Cary, Viscount Falkland," 1907, p. 248, puts it: "On the side of King Charles all the Romans and Anglicans; on that of 'King Pym' all the many varieties of Puritanism."

5. Cf. the Resolutions on Religion of February 24, 1629; reprinted in Gee and Hardy, "Documents Illustrative of English Church History," 1896, pp. 521 *sqq*.

6. A precursor of Tract No. 90, however, had been published in 1634 by "Franciscus a Sancta Clara," a pervert to Romanism of the name of Davenport, entitled "God, Nature, Grace, or a Treatise on Predestination, the Deserts and Remission of Sin,

etc., — *ubi ad trutinam fidei Catholicae examinatur confessio Anglicana et ad singula puncta quid teneat, qualiter differat, excutitur,*" etc.... A new edition of this Tract was called for in 1635. The reactionary divines meanwhile were already acting on such a theory. For the state of the case in the later years of James's reign see Bishop Carleton's "Examination of Bishop Montague's Appeal," pp. 5, 49, 94.

7. Cf. "Of Reformation touching Church-Discipline in England," 1641, p. 7; or W. T. Hale's edition, 1916, p. 8.

8. Wilkins, iv. p. 549; reprinted in Gee and Hardy, "Documents Illustrative of English Church History," 1896, p. 536.

9. Rushworth, "Historical Collections," iv. 1692, p. 93; reprinted in Gee and Hardy, pp. 537 *sq.*

10. Baillie, "Letters and Journals," ed. Laing, 1841-1842, i. pp. 273 *sq.*

11. Baillie, i. p. 303.

12. Baillie, ii. p. 117.

13. Baillie, i. p. 287.

14. The views of this party find full expression in what Mr. Marriott ("The Life and Times of Lucius Cary, Viscount Falkland," 1907, p. 197) calls Falkland's "powerful speech" in opposition to the "Root and Branch Bill." It is printed by Mr. Marriott, pp. 198-204. Falkland was a typical example of the party, says Mr. Marriott (p. 248), which "anti-Laudian but not anti-Episcopal" felt strongly the evils of the Laudian reaction but were devoted to the traditional settlement of the Church. "He is a great Stranger in Israel," said he in a speech of February 8, 1641 (Marriott, pp. 181-182), "who knows not this kingdom hath long labored under many and great oppressions, both in Religion and Liberty; and his acquaintance here is not great, or his ingenuity less, who doth not both know and acknowledge that a great, if not a principal cause of both these have been some Bishops and their adherents. Mr. Speaker, a little search will serve to find

them to have been the destruction of Unity, under pretense of Uniformity; to have brought in Superstition and Scandal, under the Titles of Reverence and Decency; to have defiled our Church by adorning our Churches; to have slackened the strictness of that Union which was formerly between us, and those of our Religion, beyond the Sea,..." and the like. The remedy, however, for these evils, he insisted, was not to take away bishops but to reduce them to their proper place and functions as spiritual officers of a spiritual body. He expresses the opinion (Marriott, p. 200) that the utter destruction of bishops was not desired by "most men," and that the petitions before Parliament were misleading, "because men petition for what they have not, and not for what they have," and the like. Yet he betrays his conviction (p. 203) that "the Scotch government" is in store for England. Similarly Baxter ("Reliquiae Baxterianae," Sylvester ed., London, 1696, I. ii. p. 146) tells us that Presbytery was "but a stranger" in England, and "though most of the ministers (then) in England saw nothing in the Presbyterian way of *practice*, which they could not cheerfully concur in, yet it was but few that had resolved on their *Principles*." He adds: [the] "most (that ever I could meet with) were against the *Jus Divinum* of Lay Elders, and for the moderate Primitive Episcopacy."

15. It was this "trenchant secularity" of Parliament—its ingrained Erastianism—which afterwards made it so earnest and persistent for the government of the Church by a Parliamentary Commission. It was in this direction that its thoughts turned at the beginning of its discussion of the settlement of the Church (see the lucid account of the debates on the Root and Branch Bill given by Shaw, "A History of the English Church, during...1640-1660," 1900, i. pp. 90 sq., and cf. Fiennes's speech, pp. 35-36); and from this determination it never receded. Mr. Marriott ("Falkland," as cited, p. 208) remarks so far justly: "The fact is that the dominant sentiment of the Long Parliament as regards the Church was neither Episcopalian, Presbyterian nor Independent;

it was Erastian. Amid infinite variety of opinions, two conclusions more and more clearly emerged: first, that there must be some form of ecclesiastical organization; and secondly, that whatever the form might be, its government must be strictly controlled by Parliament." In their Erastianism Falkland and Fiennes were wholly at one.

16. This bill was also passed by the King by a commission ("Lords' Journal," iv. p. 580), and therefore on any ground became a law of the Realm ("Statutes," v. 138; 16 Car. i. c. 27), taking effect February 13, 1642. It may be read in Gee and Hardy, p. 564.

17. The most notable early attempt to secure such advice was probably that taken by the Lords March 1, 1641, in the appointment of what has come to be known as Bishop Williams' Committee. See the full account of this Committee in Shaw's "History of the English Church, etc.," 1900, i. pp. 65 sqq.; ii. pp. 287-294; cf. A. F. Mitchell, "The Westminster Assembly "(Baird Lecture for 1882), ed. 2, 1897, pp. 100 *sqq*. Similarly, in its discussion of the "Ministers' petition and remonstrance" in February, 1641, the Commons sought the advice of divines in its committee. The desirability of a standing Assembly of Divines for giving stated advice to Parliament was adverted to by more than one speaker in the course of the discussion of the Root and Branch Bill which was introduced on May 27, 1641: on the government to be set up after the abolishing of the prelates the debaters felt the need of advice from such a body.

18. Rushworth, iv. 1692, pp. 438 *sqq*., especially p. 450; cf. Gee and Hardy, pp. 553 *sqq*., especially pp. 561 *sq*.

19. "Commons' Journal," ii. pp. 524, 535, 539, 541.

20. "Lords' Journal," v. p. 84; "Commons' Journal," ii. pp. 571, 572, 575, 579, 589, 595, etc.

21. Rushworth, v. (III. ii.), 1892, pp. 337 *sqq*.: it is printed in the preliminary materials gathered at the opening of the Scottish editions of the Confession of Faith; also in the opening pages

of A. F. Mitchell, "The Westminster Assembly," ed. 2, 1897, pp. xiii.-xvi.

22. "This is no proper Assemblie," remarks Baillie (ii. p. 186), meaning that it has no such powers as belonged to the Scottish General Assembly, "but a meeting called by the Parliament to advyse them in what things they are asked." As Dr. Leishman puts it, the Westminster Assembly "in the language of our time was rather a Parliamentary Commission The Westminster Directory, etc.," 1901, p. x.).

23. Cf. e.g. the explicit action of the Lords to this effect, "Lords' Journal," vi. p. 84, to which the closing words of the Ordinance are conformed.

24. Even the Thirty-nine Articles (Art. xxi.) declare that "General Councils may not be gathered together but by the commandment and will of princes." This was the "law of creeds" in England. Baillie (i. pp. 9546) even tells us that when the question was mooted in Scotland whether a lawful Assembly might be held without or in opposition to the will of the Crown, he was himself in grave doubt, and could find no example of a National Assembly meeting against the will of the supreme magistrate, rightly professing, either in antiquity or among the Reformed Churches. Scotland soon supplied him with an example. The doubts of Baillie in Scotland, the attitude of Parliament in England, are incident to the principle of establishment, and it would seem can finally be rid of only in free churches. We must bear in mind, however, that from the beginning the Scotch Church claimed and exercised autonomy in *spiritualia*.

25. The independence of the spirit of the Assembly is illustrated by the conflict which arose between the Assembly and Parliament in the matter of the exclusion of the scandalous from the Lord's Supper and in the much broader matter of the autonomy of the Church. In these matters, the Assembly exceeded its commission and offered unsought advice to Parliament, much

to the distaste of that body; and even declined to act on the determinations of Parliament.

26. Baillie, ii. p. 108: "Ordinarlie there will be present above three-score of their divines."

27. The House of Commons three years afterwards (December 7, 1646) sent an order to the Assembly asking to have sent up to it "all that they have done upon the Nine-and-thirty Articles," its purpose being to employ them in its negotiations with the King. After some demurring, and after attaching to them an explanatory preface, the Divines sent them up on April 29, 1647. For its own use Parliament omitted the Preface and Article viii. on the Creeds; and they were printed in this form in a tract entitled "The Four Bills, sent to the King to the Isle of Wight to be passed," which was published March 20, 1648. It is in this Parliamentary form that they have usually been reprinted, e.g. in Peter Hall's "The Harmony of Protestant Confessions," 1844, Appendix i. pp. 505-512; Neal's "History of the Puritans," ii. 1849, Appendix vii. pp. 454-457; Stoughton's "Ecclesiastical History of England," ii. ("The Church of the Commonwealth ") 1867, Appendix iii, pp. 528-535. The lacking Preface and Art. viii. are printed by Drs. Mitchell and Struthers, "Minutes of the Sessions of the Westminster Assembly of Divines," 1874, Appendix i. pp. 541-542. The complete text, with all the changes made by the Divines marked, may be found in Appendix iv. pp. 343-348 of E. Tyrrell Green's "The Thirty-nine Articles and the Age of the Reformation," London, 1896.

28. Cf. Baillie, ii. p. 177 (May 9, 1644), who, after remarking on the wide differences of opinion which emerged in the course of debate, cries out: "Had not God sent Mr. Henderson, Mr. Rutherford, and Mr. Gillespie, among them, I see not that ever they could have agreed to any settled government." The task of establishing a Presbyterian government in a Church without any experience of it, in the face of violent Independent and Erastian opposition, was no light one: and it was altogether natural that

the English divines whose Presbyterianism was purely theoretical, illuminated by no practice, should have been much disabled by varying views among themselves as to the best methods of procedure.

29. Even Dr. Shaw allows ("A History of the English Church, etc.," i. p. 3) that "it is probable that, without the necessity of calling in Scotch aid, and of adopting the Solemn League and Covenant, the Long Parliament would have resolved upon a system of Church government that might be called Presbyterian." And when he adds "though in a sense very different from that usually conveyed by the term," this caution need not be objected to: it is clear enough that the English, even in the Assembly and much more in Parliament, had much to learn as to what the Presbyterianism which they were intent on setting up was and what it carried with it. Scotch influence was necessary, however, not to make them Presbyterians, but to make them intelligent Presbyterians.

30. Cf. the "Information from the Estates of the Kingdom of Scotland to the Kingdom of England," 1640: "The second error ariseth from not knowing our laws and so measuring us with your line.... We neither know nor will examine if according to your laws these may be accounted derogatory to royal authority. But it is most sure and evident by all the registers and records of our laws...that we have proceeded at this time upon no other ground than our laws and practice of this kingdom never before questioned, but inviolably observed as the only rule of our government." The whole matter is judiciously stated by Dr. A. F. Mitchell in his Baird Lectures on "The Westminster Assembly," ed. 2, pp. 289-291; cf. W. Beveridge, "A Short History of the Westminster Assembly," 1904, pp. 116-122, note on "Spiritual Independence"; also Thomas Brown, "Church and State in Scotland," 1891, pp. 114 *sqq.*; J. Macpherson, "The Doctrine of the Church in Scottish Theology," 1903, Lectures 5 and 6.

31. Cf. the Aberdeen Articles of 1616, which the Westminster

Divines did not disdain to use in perfecting their own symbol. On these Articles, cf. C. G. M'Crie, "The Confessions of the Church of Scotland," 1907, pp. 27-35. The Articles may be read in the "Booke of the Universall Kirk of Scotland," pp. 1132-1139.

32. Cf. "Of Reformation...in England," 1641, p. 69; or Hale's ed., 1916, p. 58.

"33. Are we so modest spirits, and so towardly handlit in this matter," exclaims Baillie, when the imposition of the service-book was in progress, "that ther is apeirance we will imbrace in a clap such a masse of novelties" ("Letters," i. p. 1).

34. i. p. 18. James Gordon's account is as follows: "A number of the meaner sorte of the people, most of them waiting maides and women, who use in that towne for to keepe places for the better sorte, with clapping of their handes, cursings and outcryes, raised such .ane uncoth noyse and hubbubb in the church, that not any one could either heare or be hearde" ("History of Scots Affairs, from 1637 to 1641," 3 vols., Spalding Club, Aberdeen, 1841, i. p. 7). Cf. Balcanquhal, "A Large Declaration concerning the late Tumults in Scotland from their first Original, etc.," London, 1639, p. 23. To understand this scene we must bear in mind the division which obtained in Scotland of the Sabbath service into the Reader's and the Minister's Service. The Minister often entered the church only when his own part of the service began; and it had become the custom of "the better sorte" also to enter at that time. Meanwhile their places were kept for them by their maids. The congregation for the first half of the service was, therefore, chiefly made up of "waiting maides."

35. Baillie, i. p. 95.

36. The National Covenant is printed in the current editions of the Scottish "Confession of Faith."

37. ii. p. 90.

38. So Baillie soliloquizes ("Letters," ii. pp. 99-100): and so all men at the time judged, as even Mr. J. A. R. Marriott allows.

"Baillie is justified," says he ("The Life and Times of Lucius Cary, Viscount Falkland," 1907, p. 303) "in taking credit for the Scots in coming to the assistance of a ruined cause."

39. "Such a government shall be settled in the Church as may be... most apt to procure and preserve... nearer agreement with the Church of Scotland, and other Reformed Churches abroad." This already promised in effect the establishment of a Presbyterian system in England.

40. So Baillie, ii. p. 90; cf. also G. Burnet, "The Memoirs of the...Dukes of Hamilton, etc.," 1677, p. 237.

41. The inclusion of Ireland in the new church-system is to be observed: so that from the Treaty of Edinburgh, November 29, 1643, we hear always of "the three kingdoms" in this connection. (Cf. Shaw, "A History of the English Church, etc.," i. p. 121, note 2.)

42. Rushworth, v. 1692, pp. 478 *sq*. The "Solemn League and Covenant" is also printed in the ordinary Scotch editions of the "Confession of Faith"; and in Gee and Hardy, pp. 569 *sqq*.

43. No doubt the engagement does not in so many words bind the English to the adoption of "the Presbyterian system," and no doubt it was with a view to preserving to them a certain liberty of action that they insisted on inserting the clause "according to the Word of God," and on defining the variety of prelacy which was condemned; but much too much has been made of these things (cf. Gardiner, "History of the Great Civil War," i. 1888, pp. 270 sq.). After all the engagement bound the contracting nations to the preservation of the ecclesiastical establishment in Scotland, and to the reformation of the ecclesiastical establishment in England according to the Scotch model, so far as the Word of God permitted, and it was fully understood that whatever this saving clause denoted it had reference to details rather than to principles. It must be admitted, however, that there soon developed a disposition to treat this saving clause as permitting liberty in the settlement of the English Church, so far as the

Scriptures allowed it: and to those who were able to persuade themselves that no schedule of church government was derivable from Scripture, this liberty stretched very far. We may observe how the matter was viewed by the Parliamentary contractors, as clearly as elsewhere, no doubt, from certain words of Browne, when rebuking the Assembly (April 30, 1646) for its attitude with respect to the *jus divinum*. "It is much pressed," said he, "for the point of the Covenant. We all agree that the Word of God is the rule and must be the rule; but say there be no positive rule in the Word, are we by the Covenant bound to follow the practice of Reformed Churches in case it be against the fundamental law of the kingdom? You must interpret the Covenant so as that all parts may stand. We are bound to maintain the liberties of Parliament and kingdom. If I do any act against this I am a breaker of the Covenant" (Mitchell and Struthers, "Minutes," pp. 454 *sq*.) That is to say, Browne is so convinced that there is no divine prescription as to the government of the Church and that the sole judge in ecclesiastical things is the State, and that, as Rudyard put it on the same occasion, "the civil magistrate is a church officer in every Christian commonwealth" to whom in England all jurisdiction is reserved, that he cannot admit that the Covenant with its "according to the Word of God" imposes any form of government whatever. He has more difficulty with the adjoined phrase, "and the example of the best Reformed Churches," and in point of fact merely repudiates its binding force when inconsistent with English law—as if the very purpose of the Covenant were not to establish a new law in England. That the Covenant bound all parties to preserve the Presbyterian establishment in Scotland, no man doubted.

44. Cf. the expression given to this policy in the Preface to "The Book of Common Prayer," which was thrust upon the Scottish Church in 1637 (Professor Cooper's edition, Edinburgh and London, 1904, pp. 7-8).

45. Cf. the letter of Alexander Balfour, from Newcastle, 29 Dec., 1640, printed in Laing's ed. of Baillie's "Letters," ii. p. 473.

46. The document is printed in the Appendix to Hetherington's "History of the Westminster Assembly," ed. 4, pp. 382 *sq*. Cf. Mitchell Baird Lectures on "The Westminster Assembly," ed. 2, p. 105 and note.

47. The *jus divinum* seems to have been first claimed for Episcopacy by Bancroft in the reign of Elizabeth, but was finding many supporters at the time when Henderson's paper was drawn up, though these supporters still constituted only a party. The difference between the two parties in this matter was urged by Falkland (Marriott, p. 203): only "some bishops pretended to *jure divino*," but this is the essence of "the Scotch Government."

48. Cf. Shaw, *op. cit*., i. pp. 128-130.

49. Cf. Makower, "Constitutional History and Constitution of the Church of England," E. T. 1895, p. 78, note 37.

50. Baillie, "Letters," i. p. 365; cf. p. 376.

51. Baillie, ii. pp. 1, 2, 24.

52. Henderson's letter in Baillie, ii. p. 2.

53. Baillie, ii. p. 45.

54. Acts of Assembly, 1642 (July 22): "Acts of the General Assembly of the Church of Scotland, 1638-1842," Church Law Society edition, Edinburgh, 1843, p. 66.

55. This letter is printed in Rushworth, v. 1692, pp. 387 *sqq*.

56. Rushworth, v. 1692, pp. 390 *sqq*.

57. Baillie, "Letters," ii. p. 55.

58. These Commissioners were eight in number, and were fairly representative of the Church of Scotland, in the two parties into which it was then divided with respect to its sympathies with the old order in Scotland or with "the movement party in the South," that is, the Puritans. Robert Douglas, Alexander Henderson, Robert Baillie, with the Earl of Cassilis and Lord

Maitland, belonged to the one side; Samuel Rutherford, George Gillespie, and Archibald Johnston of Warriston to the other (cf. Leishman, "The Westminster Directory," 1901, p. ix.). Douglas and Cassilis never went up to London on their commission, which Dr. Leishman supposes to have been due to the King's veto on the Assembly, as both were strong royalists (as cited, p. x.). In the case of Douglas, at least, this seems hardly likely, in view of his position in the Commission of the General Assembly, and his letters recorded in its Minutes. Dr. Mitchell rather has the truth, when he writes (*op. cit.*, pp. 129-130): "Robert Douglas, the silent, sagacious, masterful man.... could not be spared from the duties of leadership at home, but he assisted and cheered them by his letters, maintained good understanding between them and the Church in Scotland, and in their absence came to occupy a place among his brethren almost as unique as that of Calvin among the presbyters of Geneva." The notices of his colleagues in Baillie's "Letters," which are always appreciative and affectionate, exhibit a complete harmony among the Commissioners at London; and the "Records of the Commissions of the General Assemblies of the Church of Scotland," published by Drs. Mitchell and Christie (1892), reveal an equal harmony between the Commissioners in London and the Commission in Edinburgh under the guidance of Douglas.

59. Baillie, ii. p. 84; and cf. the correspondence with the King in Rushworth, ed. 1692, III. ii. (vol. v.), pp. 393 *sq.*

60. The General Assembly ("Acts" for 1643, pp. 89-90, 90-92), addressing the *Parliament of England*, informs it that the Scottish Commissioners have been "nominated and elected" "to repair unto the Assembly of Divines and others of the Church of England, now sitting at Westminster, to propound, consult, treat, and conclude with them...in all such things...." Here the Assembly of Divines and the Scotch Commissioners are looked upon as the two parties by whose consultings together the contemplated agreements are to be reached. Addressing the

Assembly of Divines, however, the General Assembly only informs them that Commissioners had been appointed "to repair to your Assembly" without defining to what ends. It is to Parliament that the Assembly speaks as to the other contracting party.

61. This "willingness" was not, however, spontaneous. Henderson tells us (Baillie's "Letters," ii. p. 483) that the Commissioners, "against their formar resolution, were, by their friends and for the good of the cause, persuaded to joyne" with the Assembly. Baillie's own very lucid account runs as follows (ii. p. 110): "When our Commissioners came up, they were desyred to sitt as members of the Assemblie; but. they wiselie declyned to doe so: but since they came up as Commissioners for our National Church to treat for Uniformitie, they required to be dealt with in that capacitie. They were willing, as private men, to sitt in the Assemblie, and upon occasion to give their advyce in poynts debated; but for the Uniformitie, they required a committee might be appointed from the Parliament and Assemblie to treat with them thereanent. All these, after some harsh enough debates, was granted: so once a week, and whyles ofter, there is a committee of some Lords, and Commons, and Divines, which meets with us anent our commission." For this committee see p. 102.

62. "Commons' Journal," iii. p. 278; "Lords' Journal," vi. p. 265; Lightfoot's "Journal," p. 27 (xiii. 1824, of his "Works"). Cf. Baillie, ii. pp. 102, 110; and for the completeness with which they were from the first recognized and dealt with as Treaty Commissioners apart from the Assembly cf. instances in Rushworth, III. ii. (vol. v.), p. 371, ed. 1692.

63. Cf. the speech of George Gillespie in the General Assembly, August 6, 1647 (Baillie's "Letters," iii. Appendix, p. 450). "Ye know we have acted in a double capacity according to our Commission: We have gone on in a way of treating with the Committee of Parliaments and Divines jointly, and have given in many Papers, as concerning the Officers of the Kirk excluding scandalous persons from the Kirk Sacrament,

the growth of Heresies, and such things, as in your judgment and ours, was defective among them. We have acted in another capacity, debating with and assisting the Assembly of Divines their debates...." Lord Warriston thus expresses his relation to the Assembly of Divines: "I am a stranger...having a commission both from that Church and State, and at the desire of this kingdome assisting to your debats." (Speech to the Assembly of Divines, May 1, 1646, in "Records of the Commissions of the General Assemblies of the Church of Scotland," edited by Mitchell and Christie, i. 1892, p. 92.)

64. The fact that the Scotch Commissioners did not vote in the divisions of the Divines is made evident in various ways, and is confirmed by the absence of their names from all the recorded votes of the Assembly (see e.g. "Minutes," p. 252). Cf. in general the note of Dr. Mitchell in his Baird Lectures (2d ed.), pp. 180-181.

65. The order of the Commons was passed September 18 and at once communicated to the Assembly: but the Lords concurred only on October 12. See the facts drawn out by Shaw, "A History of the English Church," i. pp. 153-154.

66. "Minutes," Session 936, October 15, 1647, p. 484.

67. "Minutes," p. 484.

68. Below, pp. 36-72.

69. Originally printed in *The Princeton Theological Review*, vi. 1908, pp. 353-391.

70. Baillie, writing in 1645, says (ii. p. 320): "The bodie of the Parliament, City, and Countrey are for the Presbyterie." Cf. i. p. 287, of December, 1640: "The farr greatest part are for our discipline."

71. For example, with respect to the office of ruling elders, Baillie tells us (ii. pp. 110, 111; cf. p. 116) of the procedure thus: "Sundrie of the ablest were flat against the institution of any such officer by divine right.... The most of the synod was in our opinion.... There was no doubt but we would have carried

it by far most voices; yet because the opposites were men verie considerable, above all gracious and learned little Palmer, we agreed upon a committee to satisfie, if it were possible, the dissenters... All of them were ever willing to admitt Elders in a prudentiall way.... We trust to carie at last, with the contentment of sundrie once opposite, and silence of all, their divyne and scripturall institution." Again, more generally (ii. p. 122): "We doubt not to carie all in the Assemblie and Parliament clearlie according to our mind; but if we carie not the Independents with us, there will be ground laid for a verie troublesome schisme. Alwayes" [i.e. nevertheless] "it's our care to use our outmost endeavor to prevent that dangerous [evil]."

72. Baillie (ii. p. 307) remarks: "The most part of the House of Commons, especiallie the lawyers, whereof they are many, and divers of them very able men, are either half or whole Erastians, believing no Church-government to be of divine right, bot all to be a humane constitution, depending on the will of the magistrates." Again (p. 336), he tells us that (in 1646) two-thirds of Parliament was made up of worldly men who would have no ecclesiastical discipline if they could avoid it, Erastians, and Erastianizing lawyers, together with a small but influential band of Independents. Cf. also pp. 250, 265, 267, 277, 315. Very properly Baillie remarks therefore, that "the power of the Parliament in ecclesiastick affairs" was the greatest of the questions which were to be determined (ii. p. 205).

73. The position of Parliament laid down in the resolution with respect to the Convocation of 1640, passed December 15, 1640, *nullo contradicente*, gives a fair expression to its fundamental attitude towards all religious conventions, which was adhered to throughout. "The Clergy of England, Convented in any Convocation, or Synod, or otherwise, have no Power to make any Constitutions, Canons, or Acts, whatsoever, in Matter of Doctrine, Discipline, or otherwise, to bind the Clergy, or the Laity, of this Land, without common Consent of Parliament."

("Commons' Journal," ii. p. 51; cf. "Lords' Journal," iv. p. 273, Rushworth, iii. p. 1365.)

74. "The Pope and the King," says Baillie (ii. p. 360), "were never more earnest for the headship of the Church than the pluralitie of this Parliament."

75. "Commons' Journal," iii. p. 466; "Lords' Journal," vi. p. 525.

76. "The Form of Presbyterian Church Government": "The pastor is an ordinary and perpetual officer in the Church, prophesying of the time of the Gospel." "Votes passed in the Assembly of Divines," etc., p. 3 of "Notes of Debates and Proceedings, etc.," 1846, in Gillespie's "Works," ii. 1846: "That there is such an ordinary and perpetual office in the church as a pastor, proved, Jer. iii. 15-17 (prophesying of the time of the gospel), 1 Pet. v. 2-4."

77. "The Form, etc." "It belongs to his office, To pray for and with his flock.... To read the scriptures publickly.. . . To feed the flock, by preaching of the word.... To catechise.... To dispense other divine mysteries. To administer the sacraments. To bless the people from God.... To take care of the poor. And he hath also a ruling power over the flock as a pastor." In the "Votes," p. 3 (Gillespie, ii.): "That which the pastor is to do from God to the people," is distributed under the heads of "Reading," "Preaching" and "the dispensation of other divine mysteries"; and then "That which the pastor is to perform in the behalf and name of the people to God" is taken up and distributed into praying, ruling and caring for the poor. Under "Preaching" is subsumed both preaching and catechising; and under the general head of "the dispensation of other divine mysteries" we have the following two specifications: "That it is the office of a pastor to feed the flock by the dispensation of other divine mysteries, proved by i Cor. iv. 1, 2: the administration of the sacraments, Matt. xxviii. 19, 20; Mark xvi. 15, 16; 1 Cor. xi. 23-25, with 1 Cor. x. 16. That he is to bless the people from God, Num. vi. 23-26, with Rev.

i. 4, 5 (where the same blessings and persons from whom they came are expressly mentioned), and Isa. lxvi. 21, where, under the names of priests and Levites, to be continued under the gospel, are meant evangelical pastors, who therefore are, by office, to bless the people, Deut. x. S; 2 Cor. xiii. 14; Eph. i. 2.' The "other divine mysteries" are therefore just the Sacraments and benediction; they are enumerated as other than "reading" and "preaching" the Word.

78. Parliament was in no sense averse to a Presbyterian settlement. What it was unalterably opposed to was a *jus divinum* settlement of any kind. It was of the strongest conviction, in even its most Puritan element, that the Church derived all its authority and jurisdiction from the State; and it identified the State with itself. As Nathaniel Fiennes, son of Lord Saye, put it in the debates of February, 1641: "By the law of the land not only all ecclesiastical jurisdiction, but also all superiority and pre-eminence over the ecclesiastical state is annexed to the Imperial crown of this realm, and may be granted by commission under the Great Seal to such persons as his Majesty shall think meet." Parliament, acting as the ultimate source of authority, was to set up a government for the Church: and the government was to be the Parliament's government through and through. What government the Parliament would set up was from the first determined to be the Presbyterian. "Nor shall we need," said D'Ewes in May, 1641, "to study long for a new Church government, having so evident a platform in so many reformed churches." Only, it was Presbyterian government, not *jure divino*, but "in a prudentiall way" which was steadily contemplated. Accordingly when the "Propositions concerning Church Government" came up to Parliament this was the rock on which it struck. Parliament was very willing to order the churches on the Presbyterian model, but not to erect independent judicatories, founded in a divine right, and exercising their functions uncontrolled by Parliament. "We passed proposition 3, about which there had been some dispute

among the divines," says Whitaker ("Diary," p. 371), "with this alteration, leaving out the words, 'that the Scriptures doth hold forth,' and resolving it thus, that many several congregations may be under one Presbyterial Government." Cf. "Commons' Journal," iv. pp. 20 and 28. And when the question of the administration of the Sacrament of the Lord's Supper and the exclusion of the scandalous from it, came up, Parliament absolutely refused to commit to the church officers, in congregational or classical assemblies, the determination of what sins should be accounted scandals excluding from the Sacrament, and insisted upon itself making an enumeration of such scandals, and reserving in all other cases appeal to itself. It thus intruded into the very *penetralium* of the *spiritualia* and raised with the Assembly the precise question which Calvin had raised in Geneva in the matter of Berthelier. It was on this point that the sharpest conflict between Parliament and Assembly took place.

79. In the Elizabethan Articles of 1563, while it is asserted that "the superiority of government of all estates, and in all causes, as well ecclesiastical as temporal, within this realm" appertains to the throne, yet "the administration of the word and sacraments" is expressly excluded from the sweep of this supremacy. Parliament in 1645 was unwilling to permit even the administration of the Sacraments to remain in the unreviewed power of the ecclesiastical authorities. On the other hand, of course, the Westminster Divines in their insistence on the autonomy of the Church, were claiming far more independence of action for the Church than the Acts of Supremacy no less of the Elizabethan settlement than of that of Henry VIII allowed. The Erastian temper of Parliament, which was inclined to push the traditional control of the Church by the civil powers to extremes, was met thus by an anti-Erastian principle in the Assembly to which the old settlement seemed unendurable. There was no wish on the part of the Westminster Divines, to be sure, to take from the magistrate what is his. "We do not rob the magistrate of that

which is his," says Gillespie ("Aaron's Rod," p. xvi.), "by giving unto Christ that which is Christ's." "I do not plead against 'the power of the sword,' when I plead for 'the power of the keys.'" But they were determined that the magistrate should not take from Christ that which is His. "Is it so small a thing," asked Warriston in his speech of May 1st (see *infra*), "to have the sworde that they must have the keyes also?" This the Divines could not in conscience acquiesce in. On the Long Parliament's assumption of the entire ecclesiastical jurisdiction, see Dr. Shaw, "A History of the English Church during...1644-1660," i. 1900, pp. 227 *sqq*. ("the unscrupulous and revolutionary seizure by the Parliament of every part of the domain of ecclesiastical jurisdiction which had hitherto in whole or part belonged peculiarly to the spiritual courts," p. 236). Dr. Shaw, on the other hand, seems to consider the Parliament justified in refusing to commit to the ecclesiastical courts unreviewed powers in determining the scandals excluding from the Sacrament; which surely is a very remarkable position to take up in these later days—or at least it seems so to "the clerical mind."

80. Speech of Lord Warriston in the Assembly, May 1, 1646, in the breach of privilege matter, printed in Mitchell and Christie, "Records of the Commissions of the General Assemblies of the Church of Scotland," i. 1892, pp. 92-98 (see p. 94). Cf. W. Morison, "Johnston of Warriston," 1901, pp. 97 *sqq*.

81. "I am confident," said Warriston (see Mitchell and Christie, p. 97) to the Assembly, ". . . yee will all look and hold out the maine, Christs kingdome distinct from the kingdomes of the earth." This was said May 1, 1646. On the 6th of the previous March, the proposition "that Jesus Christ as King and Head of His Church hath appointed an ecclesiastical government in His Church in the hand of Church Officers distinct from the civil government" ("Minutes," p. 193), had been brought in for discussion; and it was vigorously debated with Coleman as the leader of the dissent until his death, at the end of March, and

then against Lightfoot through April. On July 7th it was passed with Lightfoot alone dissenting. Ultimately it was made the first paragraph of chapter xxx. of the "Confession of Faith," in the wording: "The Lord Jesus, as king and head of his church, hath therein appointed a government in the hand of church officers, distinct from the civil magistrate." This chapter was not accepted by Parliament.

82. Cf. Baillie, ii. pp. 122 *sq.*, 242.

83. See the Preface to the document (Leishman, "The Westminster Directory," pp. 9-14), and compare Marshall's explanation in the MS. "Minutes," ii. folio 2866, as quoted by Mitchell in his Baird Lectures, ed. 2, p. 240.

84. Baillie, ii. pp. 117, 131.

85. Baillie, ii. pp. 131, 140.

86. Baillie, ii. p. 148.

87. The directory for the thanksgiving after Sermon has been attributed to Dr. Edward Reynolds, from whom came also the General Thanksgiving which was added to "The Book of Common Prayer" after the Restoration (cf. E. Cardwell, "Synodalia," 1842, p. 658; Procter and Frere, "A New History of the Book of Common Prayer," 1901, p. 428; E. H. Eland, "The Layman's Introduction to the Book of Common Prayer," 1896, p. 135; L. Pullan, "The History of the Book of Common Prayer," 1905, Index, p. 330).

88. On the other hand, extemporary prayers had been prohibited on pain of deprivation in the Canons which had been imposed on the Scottish Church during the tyranny of Charles (1637). This question was a burning one.

89. Leishman, "The Westminster Directory," 1901, pp. 164, 168-169. The objection (Baillie, "Letters," ii. pp. 122-123) of the English Puritans (and the Scotch innovators, too; for this was one of "the three nocent ceremonies" objected to by them) to the minister's private prayer in the pulpit, seems to have been made insistent by an abuse of it by the prelatical party "to bow

to the east and the altar" (Baillie, ii. p. 258). It appears, however, to rest ultimately on a maxim widely adopted by the Puritans, "that all private worship in the time and place of public worship is to be discharged." The Puritans, therefore, consistently objected also to private prayers by the people on assembling for worship, and to private praying by the recipients of the Lord's Supper before and after participation. Cf. Baillie's letter to his colleagues in opposition to this sentiment, printed as Appendix E to Dr. Leishman's edition of "The Westminster Directory," pp. 188 *sqq.*; cf. also Dr. Leishman's notes, pp. 86, 132. Dr. Leishman thinks that the clause in the Directory, "Let all enter the assembly, not irreverently, but in a grave and seemly manner, taking their seats or places without adoration, or bowing themselves towards one place or other" (p. 16), does not forbid the offering of private prayer before the service has begun, but only superstitious recognition of sacred places in the sanctuary (p. 86). But it is clear that private praying on the part of late comers is forbidden in the clause: "If any, through necessity, be hindered from being present at the beginning, they ought not, when they come into the Congregation, to betake themselves to their private devotions, but reverently to compose themselves to join with the assembly in that Ordinance of God which is then in hand" (p. 17). Perhaps we may say the exception proves the rule, and the prohibition of private devotions to late comers, that they may not be inattentive to the public worship, implies the approval of private devotions for early comers, before public worship has begun. But we must have in mind also the general sentiment against such private devotions in public places. In Gillespie's notes of the debates in the sub-committee concerning the Directory ("Notes of Debates and Proceedings," etc., p. 102, in "Works," ii. 1846) we read: "Some debate was about the clause forbidding private adoration at coming into the church," which seems to imply that the purpose was to forbid all such adoration. But then it is added: "Mr. Marshall, Mr. Palmer, and others said, This is very necessary for this church, for though the minister be praying, many ignorant people will not join in it, till they have said over the Lord's prayer," which seems to suggest that late comers were at least conjointly and perhaps chiefly in mind.

90. Leishman, "The Westminster Directory," 1901, p. 17. The "Teacher" or "Doctor" was a coordinate officer with the "Pastor," which the Divines (again without the cordial assent of the Scots) found provided for in the Scriptures: "The Scripture doth hold out the name and title of teacher, as well as of the pastor; who is also a minister of the Word, as well as the pastor, and hath power of administration of the sacraments" ("Propositions for Church Government"). With respect to the difference about the "Reader," Baillie writes ("Letters," ii. pp. 122-123): "Here came the first question, about Readers: the Assemblie has past a vote before we came, that it is a part of the Pastor's office to read the Scriptures; what help he may have herein by these who are not pastors, it is not yet agitat. Alwayes [nevertheless] these of best note about London are now in use, in the desk, to pray, and read in the Sunday morning four chapters, and expone some of them, and cause sing two Psalms, and then to goe to the pulpit to preach. We are not against the ministers reading and exponing when he does not preach; bot if all this work be laid on the minister before he preach, we fear it put preaching in a more narrow and discreditable roume than we would wish."

91. This fact is adverted to by the House of Commons in the short account they gave to the Scotch Commissioners in January, 1644, of what it had already accomplished, that the Assembly in Scotland might be informed: "The Book of Common Prayer, and Festival Days, commonly called Holidays, are, by ordinance of Parliament, taken away; and a Directory for Public Worship established by the same Ordinance" ("Commons' Journal," iv. pp. 11, 12). How strong the Scotch feeling on these matters was may be hoserved from Rutherford's letter of September 23, 1637, to his parishioners at Anworth, in which he exhorts them to stand fast in the faith he had taught them (Bonar's edition, Letter 68; ed.

of 1692, Letter 148 of Part i.). Here he warns them that "no day (besides the sabbath, which is of his own appointment) should be kept holy and sanctified with preaching and the publick worship of God, for the memory of Christ's birth, death, resurrection Arid ascension; seeing such days so observed are unlawful, wil-worship, and not warranted in Christ's word." With respect to the Lord's Supper he warns them, "that ye should in any sort forbear the receiving the Lord's Supper, but after the form that I delivered it to you, according to the example of Christ our Lord, that is, that ye should sit as banquetters, at one table with our King, and eat and drink, and divide the elements one to another."

92. E.g. the American Presbyterian Churches, for whose Directory and its relations to the Westminster Directory, see L. F. Benson, in *The Presbyterian and Reformed Review*, viii. 1897, pp. 415-443.

93. In this it had a worthy forerunner in Cartwright's "Directory," a copy of which was found in his study in 1585 when he was arrested. It was reprinted in 1644 and a modern edition has been published by Principal Lorimer.

94. On the Scottish Psalter see especially J. Laing in the Appendix to his edition of Baillie's "Letters," iii. 1842, pp. 525-556.

95. Compare what they say in the Preface to their revision of the Articles ("Minutes," pp. 541-542).

96. Baillie's "Letters," i. p. 365, cf. p. 376; ii. pp. 1, 2, 24.

97. Lightfoot, xiii. p. 305—August 20, 1644; Baillie, ii. pp. 220, 221—August 18, 1644; "Minutes," p. 77, of April 9, 1645.

98. "It being necessary that the Protestant Churches Abroad, as well as the People of this Kingdom at Home, may have Knowledge how that the Parliament did never intend to innovate Matters of Faith" ("Lords' Journal," viii. p. 558).

99. An order sent to the Divines from the House of Commons July 22, 1646, urges the hastening of the Confession, and Catechism, "because of the great use there may be of them in the

Kingdom, both for the suppressing of errors and heresies, and for informing the ignorance of the people." The Divines themselves say in a petition presented to Parliament, in October, 1646: "The Confession being large, and as we conceive, requisit so to be, to setle the orthodox doctrine according to the Word of God and the Confession of the best Reformed Churches, so as to meet with common errouris" ("Records of the Commissions of the General Assemblies of the Church of Scotland," 1646-1647, edited by A. F. Mitchell and James Christie, p. 82). Cf. the speech of George Gillespie in the General Assembly, August 6, 1647 (Baillie's "Letters," ed. Laing, iii. Appendix, p. 451): "The Confession of Faith is framed, so as it is of great use against the floods of heresies and errors that overflow that land; nay, their intention of framing of it was to meet with all the considerable Errors of the present tyme, the Socinian, Arminian, Popish, Antinomian, Anabaptistian, Independent errors, etc. The Confession of Faith sets them out, and refutes them, so far as belongs to a Confession."

100. Lightfoot, xiii. 1824, p. 305; "Minutes," pp. lxxxvi. *sq.*

101. Baillie, ii. p. 266.

102. Cf. Williston Walker, "The Creeds and Platforms of Congregationalism," New York, 1893; Underhill, "Confessions of Faith...illustrative of the History of the Baptist Churches of England in the 17th Century," London, 1854; *The Presbyterian and Reformed Review*, Philadelphia, xiii. 1902, pp. 380 *sqq.* (pp. 368 sqq. of this volume).

103. *Presbyterian and Reformed Review*, October, 1901, xii. pp. 614-659; January, 1902, xiii. pp. 60-120; October, 1902, xiii. pp. 551-587.

104. Cf. *Presbyterian and Reformed Review*, April, 1902, xiii. pp. 254-276 (pp. 361 *sqq.* of this volume).

105. Cf. the statistics in the article "Puritaner, Presbyterianer," in Herzog.3 Also J. N. Ogilvie, "The Presbyterian Churches," 1897

and 1925; Henry Cowan, "The Influence of the Scottish Church in Christendom," Baird Lecture for 1895, London, 1896.

106. Cf. Mitchell, Baird Lectures on "The Westminster Assembly," ed. 2, p. 419, and the passage quoted from Heppe, p. 81.

107. An order from the Commons to hasten the Catechism had come in on July 22, 1646.

108. Writing to the Commission of the General Assembly. See the published records of the Commission, i. p. 187.

109. *Do,*: cf. "Minutes" for January 14, where the order for preparing the two Catechisms is noted and it is added that in the preparation of them, eye is to be had "to the Confession of Faith, and to the matter of the Catechism already begun" (p. 321). Cf. also Gillespie's account in his speech in the General Assembly, August, 1647 (Baillie's "Letters," iii. Appendix, p. 452).

110. It has been extracted and printed in consecutive form by W. Carruthers in his "The Shorter Catechism of the Westminster Assembly of Divines.... with Historical Account and Bibliography," London, 1897.

111. Leo Judae: "*Q.* Dic, sodes, ad quem finem homo creatus est? *R.* Ut optimi maximi ac sapientissimi Dei Creatoris majestatem ac bonitatem agnoscamus, tandemque illo Æternum fruamur."

112. Accordingly the course of salvation alone is traced in questions 20-38 with no reference whatever to the career or end of those not elected to everlasting life. The theory is that the catechumen is interested, or ought to be, exclusively in what has been done for him and what he is to expect. This is the account to give of the fact which seems strange to some (see Mitchell, Baird Lectures, ed. 2, p. 450) that there is no reference here to the future retribution of the lost. This is only a portion of a larger fact. The Catechism proceeds on the presumption that the catechumen is a child of God and gives only what the child of God needs to know of the dealings of God with him and the duties he owes to God.

113. How far this first draft may be represented by "The New Catechisme according to the forme of the Kirk of Scotland," published by the Scots in 1644 (reprinted in Mitchell's "Catechisms of the Second Reformation," 1886) we have no means of determining: but there is reason to believe that if this document was prepared by the Scots as a draft for the consideration of the Assembly, it was much departed from in the Assembly's work, which seems rather to have taken its start from Palmer's Catechism.

114. "Minutes," October 15, 1647. Before he actually took his leave (November 9), the Shorter Catechism, which ran rapidly forward, was on the point of completion. See the "Minutes" for November 8, when the Commandments, Lord's Prayer, and Creed were ordered to be added to the Catechism.

115. It would seem that the Shorter Catechism was not seriously taken in hand until October 19, 1647, and that as late as September 29, 1647, it could still seem doubtful in Scotland whether the Divines would not content themselves with the Larger Catechism. On that date the Commission at Edinburgh, acting on the assumption that there might be no Shorter Catechism prepared by the Divines, appointed a committee of its own to draw up a primary Catechism for use in Scotland. (See "Records of the Commissions of the General Assemblies, etc.," edited by Mitchell and Christie, i. 1892, p. 306.) The Assembly of Divines was already disintegrating and it was hard to get together a quorum.

116. These queries had been laid aside "till the Confession and Catechise were ended" (Baillie, "Letters," ii. pp. 379, 388), so that to return to them at this point was only to carry out a long-determined plan.

117. What was done by Parliament, however, was not little, though it was done slowly and proved not lasting. This is how it is sketched by a not very friendly hand: "The years 1640-60

witnessed the most complete and drastic revolution which the Church of England has ever undergone. Its whole structure was ruthlessly demolished—Episcopacy, the Spiritual Courts, Deans and Chapters, Convocation, the Book of Common Prayer, the Thirty-nine Articles, and the Psalter; the lands of the Bishops and of the Deans and Chapters were sold, and the Cathedrals were purified or defiled. On the clean-swept ground an entirely novel Church system was erected. In place of Episcopal Church Government a Presbyterian organization was introduced, and a Presbyterian system of ordination. For the Spiritual Courts were substituted Presbyterian Assemblies (Parochial, Classical and Provincial), acting with a very real censorial jurisdiction, but in final subordination to a parliamentary committee sitting at Westminster. Instead of the Thirty-nine Articles the Confession of Faith was introduced, and the Directory in place of the Book of Common Prayer. New Catechisms and a new metrical version were prepared, a parochial survey of the whole country was carried out, and extensive reorganization of parishes effected. Finally, the equivalent of a modern ecclesiastical commission (or let us say of Queen Anne's Bounty Scheme) was invented, a body of trustees was endowed with considerable revenues for the purpose of augmenting poor livings, and for years the work of this ecclesiastical charity and reorganization scheme was earnestly pursued. There is hardly a parallel in history to such a constitutional revolution as this...." (W. A. Shaw, "A History of the English Church during... 1640-1660," i. 1900, pp. vii.-viii.).

For additional titles
by Benjamin B. Warfield—

THE MISSION OF GREAT CHRISTIAN BOOKS

The ministry of Great Christian Books was established to glorify The Lord Jesus Christ and to be used by Him to expand and edify the kingdom of God while we occupy and anticipate Christ's glorious return. Great Christian Books will seek to accomplish this mission by publishing Gospel literature which is biblically faithful, relevant, and practically applicable to many of the serious spiritual needs of mankind upon the beginning of this new millennium. To do so we will always seek to boldly incorporate the truths of Scripture, especially those which were largely articulated as a body of theology during the Protestant Reformation of the sixteenth century and ensuing years. We gladly join our voice in the proclamations of— Scripture Alone, Faith Alone, Grace Alone, Christ Alone, and God's Glory Alone!

Our ministry seeks the blessing of our God as we seek His face to both confirm and support our labors for Him. Our prayers for this work can be summarized by two verses from the Book of Psalms:

"...let the beauty of the LORD our God be upon us, And establish the work of our hands for us; Yes, establish the work of our hands." —Psalm 90:17

"Not unto us, O LORD, not unto us, but to your name give glory." —Psalm 115:1

Great Christian Books appreciates the financial support of anyone who shares our burden and vision for publishing literature which combines sound Bible doctrine and practical exhortation in an age when too few so-called "Christian" publications do the same. We thank you in advance for any assistance you can give us in our labors to fulfill this important mission. May God bless you.

www.ingramcontent.com/pod-product-compliance
Lightning Source LLC
LaVergne TN
LVHW051014080826
845145LV00009B/2622

* 9 7 8 1 6 1 0 1 0 0 4 7 2 *